DATE DUE

Oc 10 '75	259	OCT 17 1984	1429
De 13 '75	1266	OCT 23 1985	1185
Ja 24 '76	32	1988 20	1184
Fe 6 '77	381	OCT 29 1985	2414
Oc 18 '79	1872	OCT 14 1986	1711
Se 20 '81	635	MAY 2	551
OCT 14 1982	168	Se 2 '87	562
DEC 20 1982	1061	Fe 16 '88	1252
DEC 27 1982	1081	De 23 '89	12850
JAN 17 1983	1081	Ja 16 '90	R04005D
OCT 17 1983	857	OE 3T	1219
SEP 28 1984	1429	NOV. 18 1991	1053

6

AMERICAN INDIAN TRIBES

AMERICAN INDIAN TRIBES

Marion E. Gridley

ILLUSTRATED WITH PHOTOGRAPHS AND MAPS

DODD, MEAD & COMPANY, NEW YORK

ISBN: 0-396-06985-1

Library of Congress Catalog Card Number: 74-6800
Printed in the United States of America

Acknowledgments and Credits

The author is grateful to the many persons who helped make this book possible. The photographs that appear are used through the courtesy of the following:

Alaska Visitors Association: number 79
Bureau of Indian Affairs, Department of the Interior: numbers 7, 8, 9, 10, 11, 13, 17, 20, 21, 22, 23, 24, 25, 26, 27, 28, 29, 30, 33, 34, 35, 37, 38, 41, 42, 43, 45, 46, 52, 55, 58, 70, 71, 72, 73
Dallas Morning News: number 12
National Geographic Society: number 14
Nebraska State Historical Society: number 49
New Mexico Department of Development: number 53
The Richmond Newspapers, Inc: number 3
Santa Fé Railway: numbers 2, 51, 54, 57, 59, 60, 68
State of Illinois, Department of Conservation: number 32
U.S. Department of the Interior, Indian Arts and Crafts Board: numbers 5, 6, 39, 40, 61, 62, 63, 64, 65
Western Electric: number 44

Map on pages 2-3 by Donald T. Pitcher. Map on pages 104-105 courtesy of the Bureau of Indian Affairs, Department of the Interior.

Contents

A Note from the Author

In attempting to compile lists of Indian tribes, difficulties present themselves. There are variations in spelling and in tribal identification. A tribe may be known by several other names than the name it uses for itself, and there is also confusion as to whether a group is a coalition of a number of others, whether it is a tribe, a subdivision, or an offshoot of a tribe, a band, or a village. One historian will designate a village as a tribe, depending on local importance, and another will not do so. One will spell a name phonetically and another will use some other form of spelling. Within an area, a tribe might be called one name by the English and another by the French, and still another by other Indians. Some of the variances come about because of differences in dialects.

To illustrate, the Mohicans are also known as the Mahicans and the Mohegans. These Indians occupied both sides of the upper Hudson River in New York almost to Lake Champlain. They were also in the upper part of the Housatonic Valley in Massachusetts and along the Connecticut River. The name, in a variety of forms, was applied to those living along the Hudson. Those on the lower Hudson were called the Mahican, and those along the Connecticut River were the Mohegan. The French called these Indians the Loups, and this name often appears on old maps.

The Hurons were so-called by the French, but they called themselves the Wendots, which later became Wyandotte or Wyandot. The Chippewa in Canada are the Ojibwa. The name Menominee is also spelled Menomini, and Navajo is frequently spelled Navaho. But the Navajos do not call themselves by this name; they are the Diné. The Kalispels are known to the French as the Pend d'Oreilles.

There was considerable shifting about within a region and forming and reforming of a confederacy or coalition. There was overlapping from one region to another, and there was crisscrossing over both the Canadian and Mexican borders.

In this book, the effort has been to list only those groups considered distinct tribes. In cases where there is some cloudiness between a village and a tribe, the name was not included, and, unless a subdivision was very important in its own right, it was not included. Where there were mergers, the larger tribe merged into is included, but not always those smaller ones that merged into it. Some tribes now extinct are included if they were of some degree of importance in their day. There were very many small units and not all of these are included, for there would be far too many.

As nearly as possible, the tribes are located according to their original dwelling place. Where overlapping occurs, they are listed in each region occupied. When they lived, or are living, in an area that is not native to them, this is indicated with an asterisk. Reservation lists show the locations of tribes today, and also included are the non-reservation groups and communities—the remnants of tribes that departed from the area or were destroyed by war and disease.

For example, there are still Creeks living in Alabama on land given to one of their leaders, who had once saved the life of Andrew Jackson, by the government. They are completely independent, although they have shared in the distribution of recent monies paid to the Creek tribe in settlement of land claims against the government. The Ottawas living in Michigan are descendants of those who did not go west with the tribe. There are very many tribes in Oklahoma which were relocated from their original territories and which do not now live on reservations.

The family, or language, stocks are not restricted to a region, but have a wide and far range over the country. Athapascans of the far north are found also in the Southwest. The Algonquians are widespread. There are Siouans in the East, but most are on the Plains. Major linguistic stocks within a region have been listed. Again, spellings may vary and names may differ from those in other books. Those used here are as they are given in the working list for anthropological students as provided by the Smithsonian Institution in the *Handbook of American Indians*.

—M.E.G.

AMERICAN INDIAN TRIBES

Indian Tribes in General

America is a land of many features. It is a country of woods and plains, deserts and mountains. In each of these differing regions, Indian people lived and their whole way of living was influenced by the environment in which they were placed. This was the natural response to the material things which were at hand for use and to the physical conditions of their surroundings.

Although there was a general life-style in each of the various regions, there was no one single language and it was impossible, in many instances, for one tribe to understand the language of another. Indians are classified according to language and other similarities into groupings known as linguistic or family stocks, and also by regional culture areas. The list of linguistic or family stocks is fairly long, but the single largest language group is the Algonquian. Culture areas are geographical divisions, such as the Eastern Woodlands, Plains, Southwest, or Northwest Coast.

Indian tribes were made up of clans which were family, or kinship, units. A number of families formed a band, and a number of bands formed a tribe. But the term "tribe" had no uniform application. There were confederacies, with dominant tribes and subordinate ones. There were governmental

1

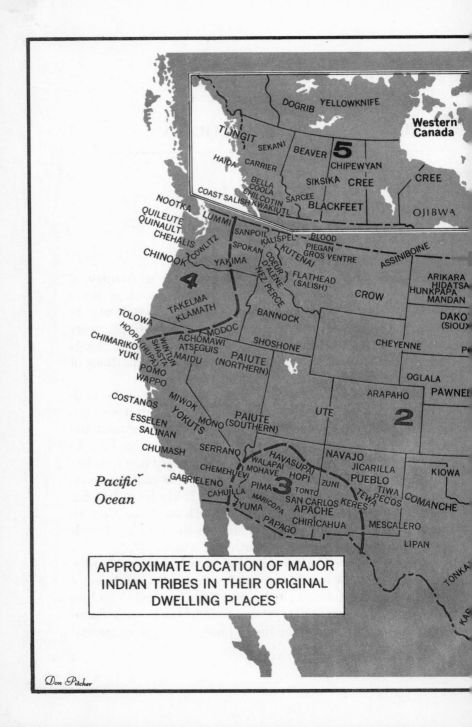

APPROXIMATE LOCATION OF MAJOR
INDIAN TRIBES IN THEIR ORIGINAL
DWELLING PLACES

Don Pitcher

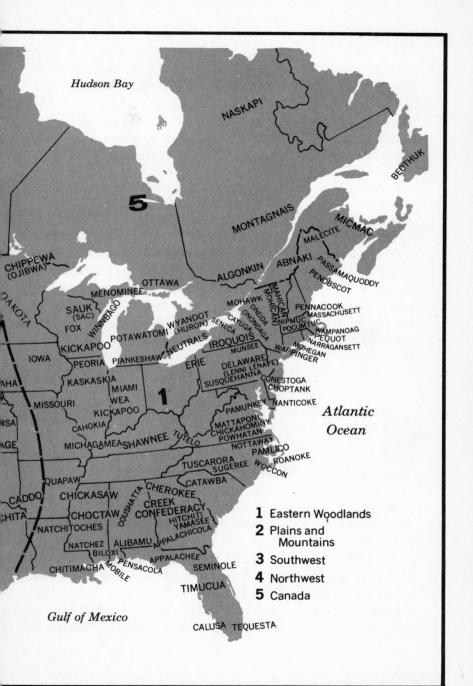

confederations, such as the Iroquois Confederation, with tribes only a part of the governing unit. There were nations, villages, and communities. It is only possible to guess at the number of tribes and the number of Indians found in this country at the time Columbus came to America. There are approximately 250 tribes today and an estimated 800,000 or more Indians.

Some of the earlier tribes were destroyed by wars among themselves, or by plagues which swept the country, and had vanished from the scene by the time of colonization by white men. Others were destroyed or cut down in wars with the settlers, or by cruelties inflicted upon them by the various incoming groups who saw them as inferior people standing in the way of settlement, or as people to be played against each other and used in the drive for power and conquest by the European factions. Or, as people to be exploited and despoiled of their natural riches in resources. The land of this country was not always obtained from the original owners with honor and we who occupy it today have much with which to reproach ourselves.

Indians of today live largely on reservations, mostly west of the Mississippi. Reservations are not "concentration camps," as they are frequently labeled. Indians have complete freedom of movement, leaving or returning at will. There are also non-reservation communities in various parts of the country, the remnants or remainder groups of once powerful or large tribes of the area. (The reservation lists herewith indicate the locations of major tribes today, listing both reservations and non-reservation groups.)

Most reservations are under the administrative jurisdiction of the Bureau of Indian Affairs, an agency of the government in the Department of the Interior. Today, most reservations are governed by Tribal Councils elected by the members of the tribe, with final approval of certain actions remaining in the hands of the Interior Department and Congress. This means that Indians are not entirely independent in the management of their affairs, but there is a growing trend for tribes to take over the management of the reservation completely, with the guidance of the Bureau of Indian Affairs available when needed or requested. The status of Indian lands changes from time to time. Reservations and trust lands may be terminated as such and administrative jurisdiction shifted. The map showing the location of Indian reservations was prepared by the Bureau of Indian Affairs in 1971.

The government provides schools for Indians both in reservation and non-reservation situations, educational scholarships for higher learning, vocational and adult training. Again, the trend is for the tribes to take over the management and operation of Indian schools. Hospital and medical care is provided for Indians without charge, through the Indian division of the U.S. Public Health Service, which also operates a recruitment program to draw Indians into medical and health professions.

Through the industrial division of the Bureau of Indian Affairs, Indians are attempting to interest industries in locating on or near reservations and to train Indian labor. The established industrial projects, which cover a wide range of activities, are operating very successfully and have opened new avenues of vocations and employment. Indians are also establishing tourism facilities on their reservations and operate motels, camp sites, spas, ski grounds, restaurants, and recreational areas which are also revenue- and employment-producing.

Some tribes, although they live on reservations, do not come under the federal bureau, but under the states of their location. Other Indians live in small communities or settlements and are on their own. Very many now live in the large cities, drawn there by employment opportunities.

Numbers of Indian tribes have mineral, oil, timber, grazing lands, cattle herds, and other assets. Some tribes are quite wealthy. But even among tribes with wealth, there can be pockets of extreme poverty among individuals, and there are tribes that of themselves are extremely poor. The development of natural resources is being actively explored.

Most Indian tribes, both east and west of the Mississippi, live in the area of their original homelands. Those in Arizona and New Mexico have been desert dwellers for thousands of years. The principal exceptions to this statement would be certain tribes in Oklahoma, Kansas, and Nebraska who were moved to their present locations.

Original customs and religions have very largely been lost except for the groups of traditionalists who preserve and practice them. In the Southwest, Indian custom and tradition is strongly entrenched, though even there it is changing as the older people die or as modernism alters conditions. There is respect and love for the old traditions, however, and a movement to restore ancient religious beliefs is gaining ground as a means of retaining Indian identity.

For the modern "powwows," customs and costumes are largely borrowed from the Indians of the Plains. It is not possible to say that something is *the* Indian way," or *the* Indian belief," or *the*" Indian anything. There was no such thing. Each tribe was individualized in its beliefs and ways, and one can say only, "This is from the Hopi, or the Sioux, or the Choctaw," depending on what is being discussed.

Indians of the Eastern Woodlands

The Indians of eastern America were woodland people. They were primarily agricultural, but they were also hunters and fishermen.

Those who lived in the coastal states were the first to come in contact with the Europeans, and this was long before the arrival of Columbus. The Norsemen came to North America some five hundred years before, and fishing vessels from other countries later explored and traveled the shoreline.

When the eastern Indians were first contacted, they were still living in the Stone Age. Houses were made of an open framework formed by saplings set firmly in the ground, bent over and tied at the top in the form of a round lodge or an oval one like an arbor. These frameworks were covered with mats of bark or of woven rushes. The dome-shaped houses held a single family and were called *wigwams*. Long, barn-like structures, built in a similar manner, were called *long houses* and held from five to twenty families. Some villages composed of these houses were often fortified and surrounded by stockades.

In the warm South, the houses were open shelters with thatched roofs. In most villages, especially in the South, the houses were grouped around a central square where games and ceremonies were held. In the southern villages, too, there was a temple building for religious rites.

The eastern Indians were known as Woodland Indians because they lived in wooded country and their culture was based on the use of bark and wood for household utensils, implements, and weapons, for basket weaving and for tieing materials. Decorative designs were influenced by the patterns of the woods—the leaves, flowers, and vines. Some implements and weapons were made of stone, and of shell in the Deep South.

The woods were alive with game and fur-bearing animals which provided food and clothing; rivers and lakes teemed with fish and the ocean with oysters, clams, and other shellfish. The Indians of the Atlantic seaboard did not go out upon the ocean for sea hunting, like the tribes of the Pacific coast. They did not have the huge trees from which to make seagoing vessels. Instead, their boats were the birchbark or dugout canoes, light and graceful but far from sturdy. For winter travel, snowshoes and toboggans were made.

Wild plants, fruits, berries, and nuts grew in profusion, and in the northern woods sugar was made from the sap of maple trees. In the far South, a good food came from the palm tree. In their gardens, the eastern Indians planted corn, beans, pumpkins, squash, and sunflowers for the rich oil which came from the seeds. They also raised tobacco, which was considered sacred.

More than any other tribes—with the exception of those of the Northwest—the chiefs of the eastern Indians were acknowledged as rulers and the chieftainship was hereditary. Even so, the chief had no rights or privileges above others, but dedicated his life to his people and their welfare. While there were some matters in which he could act independently, he generally did not do so, but met in council with the headmen of his tribe before coming to a decision. The chief was a leader rather than a dictator. The one who inherited the title, or was elected to it—where election was the rule —had to prove himself worthy of it and could be challenged and removed if he did not.

Indians of New England

The New England states were well populated with Indians. Mostly, there were small bands or branches of larger groups, joined in a loose relationship with one strong tribe for protection.

In the list of area tribes which is given, they are located according to their main base. But all of them wandered through the neighboring country and were found scattered about other places. They usually moved several times each year in the quest for food. Each spring they fished in the rivers and planted their gardens along riverbanks. By June, they moved to the coast where they hunted eggs and the young of seabirds, gathered clams, oysters, and lobsters, drying some for winter use. With the first sign of frost, they returned to the rivers to harvest their crops, and in October moved farther upstream to hunt the forests for big game. A two-week Thanksgiving feast was held in late November or early December, and the winter months were spent in hunting deer or moose in the far north, and trapping small game. The spring catch of otter and beaver was made before the ice left the rivers, and when the water was ice-free, muskrat trapping took place and the cycle of fishing and planting began once more.

There were no Indians living in Vermont except in a very small portion of it. The mountains were a barrier between the New England groups and the Iroquois farther south. Vermont was used as hunting territory by various bands, however.

All of the New England tribes were of the Algonquian linguistic stock. People frequently confuse the Algonquians and call them a tribe, but there was no tribe by this name. (The name Algonkin was used for a small band of Indians in Canada who were actually the Weskarini and who lived along the Ottawa River in Quebec. The name was also used for a grouping of very small bands at one time, and Algonkin is probably the name from which the name of the great Algonquian linguistic stock was derived.)

Many of the New England tribes had disappeared before the Pilgrims came, because of epidemics of plague. Hundreds of others were destroyed in wars between themselves or with the colonists. Only in Maine did the Indians successfully withstand the settlers, and this was because they were under the protection of French missionaries.

Of the Maine Indians, the Abnaki were important. About thirteen or more smaller groups formed the Abnaki Confederation. The Abnaki tribe proper was first visited by Verrazano in 1524. In 1604, they were visited by Champlain and from then on were an important factor in the history of the region which was to form the state of Maine.

The Abnakis were closely attached to the French and were greatly influenced by them. Because of this, they fought continuously with the English, who were seeking to establish themselves in the New World and to end French domination of it. When warfare broke out in 1675, there were about 6,000 English settlers in Maine. In a period of eighty-five years, there were six Indian wars. Two of these lasted ten years, and the rest six years each or less. The first three saw much aggressive Indian action and the near ruin of the fur, fishing, and lumber business for the English. But Indian strength was exhausted in this fighting, and in the last three wars the English took over the aggressive role, raiding many Indian villages and camps. The French, who had openly helped the Indians, made peace with the English after the last Indian war. Their power in the New World was over. The Abnakis then gradually withdrew to Canada. Their descendants live today near the city of Quebec.

The Passamaquoddy, with the Malecite, were sometimes called the Etchimins. The Passamaquoddy were the largest group of the Abnakis, but they were not a large tribe. However, they were able to remain in their homeland in Maine where they now have two reservations.

At the time of the American Revolution, Maine was a district of the Bay Colony of Massachusetts. The Passamaquoddy, at the urging of General George Washington, won a number of victories over the English. In 1794, they entered into a treaty with Massachusetts by which millions of acres of Indian lands were ceded. The Passamaquoddy retained approximately 24,000 acres, which are their present holdings.

The Penobscot tribe was the largest one in Maine. It is not certain whether this was also an Abnaki group, for it acted independently of them, but they are listed as such. The Penobscots were active in all of the Maine wars until 1794 when a treaty of peace was consummated. This angered the Abnakis, who still fought in the interests of the French, and a breach developed. Because of this, the Penobscots did not go to Canada when the Abnakis did.

In final land settlements, the Penobscots were given rights to some 140 islands in the Penobscot River, totaling in all some 4,500 acres. The Penobscots still live in this area, their largest village on Indian Island near Old Town. Some live in Bangor or in other parts of the state.

Of this tribe, Chief Orono was once an important historic figure. He became prominent after he reached the age of fifty, and he did not become head chief until he was seventy-five. At the beginning of the French and Indian War against the English, Orono strongly advocated peace. At the beginning of the Revolution, he offered his services to the Massachusetts colonists and proved to be a faithful ally during the struggle for independence. When he was one hundred and eight years old, he entered into treaties with Massachusetts, which fixed the permanent title to the Penobscot Reservation. The town of Orono is named for him and there is a memorial there in his honor.

In a later day, another Penobscot of note was Louis Sockalexis, who was the first full-blooded Indian to play professional baseball. He played outfield with the Cleveland Indians and it is said that the team was named for him.

From Maine, also, came Samoset, who did much to shape the history of America. Samoset was a chief whose village occupied the present site of Bristol. It is not clear from which tribal group he came, but he was most likely an Abnaki. Samoset was the first Indian to meet the Pilgrims. Striding boldly down the main street of Plymouth, his hand raised in greeting, he called out, "Welcome, Englishmen!" He had learned to speak English from the crews of fishing boats which frequentd the coastal waters.

It was Samoset who brought Squanto to Plymouth to be the friend and benefactor of the Pilgrims, and who arranged for them to meet with Massasoit, the great chief of the Wampanoags. From this meeting came a treaty of peace which lasted for forty years.

Each of the three Maine reservations elects a governor, lieutenant governor, and a tribal council. Both tribes send a representative to the state legislature but without voting or other privilege. Maine is the only state to have a State

Department of Indian Affairs. The director of this is John Stevens, a Passamaquoddy, who was elected governor of his tribe when he was twenty years old and held that office for seventeen years.

In New Hampshire, the Pennacook Confederacy included sixteen tribes, with the Pennacook the largest. The New Hampshire groups were all quite small. In 1633–34 many of them died in a plague which swept New England, and they were never again very strong. A few Pennacooks still live in New Hampshire near the town of Manchester, but there are no full-blood Indians among them.

Vermont's only Indians, the Missiassik or Missisquoi, moved to Quebec in 1730.

Massachusetts was named for the tribal confederacy, said to have had 3,000 warriors and more than twenty villages before the coming of the Pilgrims. By the time the Pilgrims arrived, these Indians had been nearly destroyed in a war with the Abnaki. Others died in the plague epidemic. The tribe disappeared around 1650.

The principal tribe in Massachusetts was the Wampanoag, with thirty villages and in control of all of southern New England. The English people were not unknown to Massasoit, the chief, because in 1605 five of his young braves were kidnapped and taken away by an English sea captain. One of these five was Squanto, from the village of Patuxet, who was the first American to cross the Atlantic four times.

Squanto lived in England nine years after his first kidnapping. He returned to America with Captain John Smith, but soon after his arrival was kidnapped again. He returned to America in 1619, only to find that his entire village had died when the plague struck. He was without friends or relatives.

It was on the site of Patuxet that the Pilgrims were to settle when they arrived the following year. Squanto adopted the Pilgrims, as they adopted him. He did not hate them because he had been kidnapped and taken far away from his home. He loved them because English people had been kind to him when he lived among them.

When Squanto came to Plymouth, the Pilgrims had struggled through a terrible winter. They had been overcome by illness, were starving and without hope. Squanto taught them many things so that they were able to live, and to thrive, in the wilderness. He lived in the home of Governor Bradford and when he died, two years after the Pilgrims came, he bequeathed all of his simple possessions to Bradford and begged him to pray that he would enter heaven.

Squanto was the interpreter in the meeting that took place with Massasoit and for the drawing up of the peace treaty. It was agreed in the treaty that the two peoples would not harm each other and that they would aid each other in time of distress.

The Wampanoags thus became the first Indian tribe to sign the first treaty of peace ever made on New England soil, the first to negotiate a land title in this country, and the first to make a gift of many acres of land to an English king. Massasoit acknowledged that the King of England would be the supreme ruler of the country and as his first royal gift presented the king with hundreds of acres of Massachusetts lands.

It was with Massasoit and the Wampanoags that the first Thanksgiving feast was held. It is said that the Indians introduced popcorn to the Pilgrims at the Thanksgiving celebration.

In time, the Wampanoag villages were nearly surrounded by the expanding white settlements. Massasoit's sons, Wamsutta and Metacom, fretted over this encroachment on Indian lands and the unfair treatment that they saw take place, but Massasoit steadfastly clung to his friendship with the English. He had given them his word, and further, the English protected the Wampanoags from the hostile tribes to the north. He was glad to be secure in the heart of the English settlements.

With Massasoit's death, Wamsutta became chief and continued the friendly relationship. But he, too, died shortly after assuming the chieftainship. Believed to be plotting against them, the English placed Wamsutta under arrest and he died on the way to Plymouth. All of the Indians believed that he had been poisoned.

Metacom, who had the English name of Philip, was now the leader. He was called King Philip after the English custom. Indians did not have titles or concepts of royalty. Because of their association with the English, however, such titles came into use among eastern tribes and are still in use in some areas today.

The colonists had grown independent and the Indians were no longer of value in the support of their economy. They became intolerant of the Indians and arrogant in their treatment of them, and the friendly ties that had once existed were broken.

Philip worked secretly in an attempt to form a coalition of all of the tribes of New England, and he planned that they would strike all at the same time in a war that would drive the whites out of the land. This was excellent strategy and proved Philip to be an unusual leader, but it was difficult to accomplish. Indians were accustomed to acting and fighting as individual tribes and not under a single leader. Had Philip brought about his goal, it is quite probable that he would have succeeded in his purpose as well.

When the war finally broke out, Philip was not quite prepared, but he was better prepared than the English, who were widely scattered. Philip had to act, because his plot had been betrayed by a Christianized Indian. Once the fighting was in progress, some of the other tribes fell into line and

Philip's final victory seemed almost certain. Then the English began to organize their fighting ranks, and with this, the tide turned against the Indians.

Philip was eventually killed in a fight in a swamp near Mount Hope in Rhode Island. He was beheaded and his head displayed on a pole at Plymouth for twenty-four years. His wife and child were sold as slaves in the West Indies.

For a time, the few remaining Wampanoags tried to hold together. Then they, too, acknowledged defeat and went to live on small reservations. These were eventually taken over by the state of Massachusetts. Some of the people stayed in the fishing ports and the men became sailors. There are no pure-bred Wampanoags living today, but there are descendants on Martha's Vineyard and Cape Cod, and in some of the Massachusetts towns.

The Stockbridge Indians were a tribe of the Mahican (Mohegan) Confederacy that lived in Massachusetts. Because they were allies of the English, they were constantly set upon by the French in early colonial times. At the end of the French and Indian War, only 200 Stockbridges were alive. Joining the Wappinger, they fought for the Americans during the Revolution, and in 1785 moved to the Oneida Reservation in New York. In 1833 they removed, with the Oneidas and a few Munsee, to Wisconsin where they have a small reservation.

In 1660, a reservation was set aside in Massachusetts for any Christianized Indians that sought refuge there. These Indians became known as the Mashpee. They have four small communities in Massachusetts today.

Of those tribes living in Connecticut, the Pequots were by far the most important. Numbering about 3,000, the Pequots controlled the eastern part of the state. At one time, the Pequots and the Mohegans (Mahicans) were one tribe. They were divided when Uncas rebelled against the Pequot chief,

Sassacus, and left with his followers. Uncas was made famous by James Fenimore Cooper in his book *The Last of the Mohicans*. In this story, Uncas is "glamorized" so that he does not resemble his true character.

In 1637, the Pequots were nearly destroyed by the white colonists. The few survivors tried to find a haven among the Mohawks, who put them all to death. This strengthened the position of the Mahicans who now became the only Indians of importance in southern New England after King Philip's War. Gradually they sold their lands and removed to Wisconsin where only a hanndful now live.

Two descendants of Uncas—Gladys and Harold Tantaquidgeon—have constructed a replica of a Mohegan village at Uncasville, Connecticut. They have a museum of Indian relics, and both entertain visitors with descriptions of tribal history and custom. Gladys Tantaquidgeon is an anthropologist who has her degree from the University of Pennsylvania.

Samson Occom, another descendant of Uncas, was one of the outstanding Indians of his day. When he was about seventeen, Samson studied under the Reverend Eleazer Wheelock, who had a small school for the education of Indians. Samson became an ordained Congregational minister and teacher, and he was sent to England to raise funds to assist Wheelock's Indian school. He gave between three hundred and four hundred sermons there and returned with some eleven thousand English pounds. With this money, Dartmouth College was founded. In Occom's honor, Dartmouth established an Indian education policy which for many years provided free education to any qualified Indian wishing to enroll there.

The Connecticut General Assembly has now approved the creation of an Indian Affairs Council within the Department of Environmental Protection. Representatives from the four

Indian reservations will act as advisers to the non-Indian board.

A bill has also been submitted in the Massachusetts Legislature which authorizes the establishment of a Commission to meet with the Nipmucs and Wampanoags over lands seized in that state by eminent domain. The Indians intend to claim every piece of land for which they can find proof and any land for which the state cannot produce a deed. Thousands of acres will come under investigation, including lands on which cities have been built.

The Narragansetts were one of the largest and strongest of the New England tribes and the major group in Rhode Island. They numbered several thousand when the Pilgrims came, and added to this number by absorbing the remnants of those groups struck down by the plague.

Siding with King Philip, the Narragansetts were as shattered by his war as were the Wampanoags. In the Battle of the Great Swamp, in which the most savage fighting of the war took place, the tribe was nearly annihilated. A thousand or more of their warriors were killed.

The Indians who are survivors of the Narragansetts have not forgotten that terrible battle. They have established on its site a shrine to brotherhood, and a pilgrimage is made each September to the spot. Ceremonies are held around the monument standing there, and the people circle this monument carrying flowers to form a living wreath.

Princess Gladys Redwing, who has been the prime mover in keeping the Narragansett memory alive among the 1,000 or so of the tribe still living in Rhode Island, has, with her family, established an inn, a restaurant serving Narragansett foods, and a museum. The complex is highly popular with tourists. During the year, special Narragansett feasts are held, and those interested are taken to see the site of Great Swamp, and to hear the story from those who know it by tradition.

TRIBES OF NEW ENGLAND

(Maine, New Hampshire, Vermont, Massachusetts, Rhode Island, Connecticut)

Abnaki Confederacy

Abnaki ("east land people")	Maine
Amaseconti ("abundance of small fish")	Maine
Arosaguntacook	Maine
Malecite	Maine
Micmac	Maine (border)
Missiassik	Lake Champlain, Vermont
Norridgewock ("people of the still water between rapids")	Maine
Passamaquoddy ("plenty of pollock")	Maine
Penobscot ("plenty stones")	Maine
Pequawket ("at the hole in the ground")	Maine, New Hampshire
Rocameca ("on the land upstream")	Maine
Sokoki ("people at the outlet")	Maine
Wawenoc ("people of the bay country")	Maine

Pennacook Confederacy

Accominta ("shoreline")	Maine
Agawam ("fish-drying place")	Massachusetts
Amariscoggins	New Hampshire
Amoskeag ("one who takes small fish")	New Hampshire
Coosuc ("at the pine")	New Hampshire
Nashua ("the land between")	Massachusetts
Newichawanoc	Maine
Ossipee ("lake made by river widening")	Maine
Pemigewasset	New Hampshire
Pennacook ("people at bottom of the hill")	New Hampshire
Piscataqua	New Hampshire
Souhegan	New Hampshire
Squamscot	New Hampshire
Wachuset ("at the small mountain")	Massachusetts
Wamesit	Massachusetts
Winnecowet	New Hampshire
Winnipisawki	New Hampshire

Wappinger Confederacy

Mattabesee ("great rivulet")	Connecticut
Paugusset ("where the narrows open out")	Connecticut
Quinnipiac ("long water people")	Connecticut
Siwanoy ("salt people")	Connecticut, New York
Tankiteke	Connecticut, New York
Tunxis ("the point where the river bends")	Connecticut
Uncowa ("beyond")	Connecticut
Wecquaesgeek ("end of the marsh")	Connecticut, New York

Nipmuc Confederacy

Nipmuc ("fresh-water fishing place")	Massachusetts, Connecticut
Quabaug ("red pond")	Massachusetts
Quinebaug ("long pond")	Connecticut
Wunnashowatuckong ("people at the fork of the river")	Massachusetts
Wusquowhananawkit ("at the pigeon country")	Massachusetts

Mahican (Mohegan) Confederacy

Mahican ("wolf")	Connecticut, Massachusetts
Stockbridge	Massachusetts

Wampanoag Confederacy

Nauset	Massachusetts
Patuxet	Massachusetts
Wampanoag ("eastern people")	Massachusetts

Miscellaneous Tribes

Mashpee ("great pond")	Massachusetts
Massachusett ("at the great hill")	Massachusetts
Montowese ("little god")	Connecticut
Namoskeags	New Hampshire
Nantucket	Nantucket Island
Narragansett ("people of the small point")	Rhode Island

Niantic ("a point of land on an estuary")	Rhode Island, Connecticut
Nonotuc	Massachusetts
Norwootuc	Massachusetts
Pequot ("destroyers")	Connecticut
Pocumtuc	Massachusetts
Podunk ("a neck of land")	Connecticut
Poquonnoc ("a clearing")	Connecticut
Pyquag ("open country")	Connecticut
Scaticook (Schaghticoke) ("at the river fork")	Connecticut
Squawkeag	Massachusetts
Sukiaug	Connecticut
Wabaquasset	Connecticut

Major Linguistic Stock
Algonquian

INDIAN RESERVATIONS IN NEW ENGLAND

MAINE

Passamaquoddy	Washington county (two reservations)
Penobscot	Penobscot county

CONNECTICUT

Schaghticoke	Litchfield county
Golden Hill (Paugussett)	Fairfield county
Western Pequot	New London county
Eastern Pequot	New London county

Non-reservation Communities

MAINE

Malecite	Aroostook county

NEW HAMPSHIRE

Pennacook	Hillsboro county

MASSACHUSETTS

Mashpee	Barnstable, Bristol counties
Nipmuc	Worcester county
Wampanoag	Martha's Vineyard Island
Mixed tribes	Plymouth, Norfolk counties

CONNECTICUT

Mohegan	New London county

RHODE ISLAND

Narragansett	Washington, Providence counties

Indians of New York State

Of the Indians of New York State, the greatest, most powerful, and most well-known were those of the Iroquois Confederacy. In statesmanship and in war, they stood above all others and no tribe north of Mexico ever equaled them.

The Confederacy is traditionally said to have been founded in the 1500's by Dekanawida. At that time there was much fighting among the Indians and they were being reduced to starvation by the continuous battles. Dekanawida dreamed of a great plan for peace and he spent some time among various tribes in hopes of finding acceptance of his dream. He enlisted Hayenwaten, a Mohawk, as a disciple and Jokonsaseh, a Seneca, who was known as the Peace Queen. Hayenwaten, also called Hiawatha, is often confused with the Hiawatha of Longfellow's poem. But Longfellow's Hiawatha was fictional and largely borrowed from Chippewa mythology, and Hayenwaten was a real person who successfully joined the original five tribes into a confederacy for peace. Later, when the Tuscaroras migrated to New York from North Carolina, they were adopted into the Confederacy, which then became the League of Six Nations. It has been called the first League of Nations. Because they lived in long bark houses, and because their territory stretched

from east to west like a long house, the Iroquois called themselves "People of the Long House."

The Iroquois Indians are of Iroquoian family, or linguistic,
stock. There are other tribes in this family, and some of them
quite important, but generally, when Iroquois Indians are
referred to, the reference is to those comprising the League.

The Iroquois held the balance and control of the entire
New York State area and their power extended even further
in all directions. Strong allies of the English, it was they who
prevented the French from coming south of the St. Lawrence
River or penetrating the interior country.

The decisions made in the Iroquois councils were so necessary to the expansion plans of the countries seeking to establish themselves in the New World that they were reported
and discussed with great seriousness in the royal courts of
Europe. Iroquois chiefs were taken on jaunts to these countries where they were treated as royalty and avidly courted
by those who vied to dominate America. They were also
wooed by the various colonies.

With the outbreak of the American Revolution, the Iroquois League came to an end. It was a rule of the Confederacy that all action must be the result of the unanimous
vote of the council of chiefs. In the intense debate which took
place over where Indian loyalties should remain in that war,
three of the tribes were strongly tied to the English while
the Oneidas and Tuscaroras wished to embrace the American cause. It was impossible to arrive at a unanmious decision
and so the League had to be dissolved if the tribes were to
go their separate ways. So the great Confederacy, which had
reigned as lords of the forest, came to an end.

England had always dealt with the Indians as sovereign
nations with the right to occupy the lands on which they
lived. The Americans considered the Iroquois as English subjects. To the despair of the Indians, England had now aban-

doned them. In the treaty of peace that was made between the king and the "thirteen fires," no provision of any kind was made for the Indians, although they had rendered valuable services to both sides.

The Mohawks fled to Canada where they were settled on two reservations. The one near Montreal extends over the border into New York. The Senecas pledged their loyalty to the United States, and were followed by the other tribes and in return for this all were allowed to keep their New York lands after ceding large portions of them. They remained loyal Americans and refused to help England in the War of 1812.

Because George Washington was sympathetic to their plight and permitted them to remain in New York when he could have exiled them, the Senecas honored him, and still do. George Washington, it is said, lives in the Seneca heaven. He has a beautiful mansion surrounded by lovely gardens, standing at the entrance to "the land in the sky." Washington is the only person not an Iroquois who is permitted to live there.

New York State is responsible for all programs for Indian welfare and all Indian children attend public schools. Indians may cross the Canadian border at will without restriction or interference.

The Senecas have had a constitutional form of government incorporated in New York since 1849. The city of Salamanca is on Seneca property and is leased by the Indians to the townspeople.

Many Mohawks live in Brooklyn in an area called the "Gowanus district." These are the skilled high-steel workers, who find steady employment and high salaries in the construction of our tallest buildings. Mohawks got into this type of work by accident. They had no fear of "cat walking" along

steel girders or of working at dizzying heights, and this type
of work became a tribal vocation. Mohawks were employed
on the Empire State Building and the Mackinac and Verrazano bridges, among others. With a few individual exceptions, the Mohawks are the only Indians to follow this
dangerous vocation as a tribe.

There are many outstanding Iroquois, both in history and
in modern life. In the Revolutionary War period, Joseph
Brant (Thayendanega) and Red Jacket were the most
noted. Brant, the most famous of all, was the first Mohawk
to read and write. He was educated in the mission school
which was later to become Dartmouth College. Brant did
more than any other Indian to hold his people loyal to England, and he was commissioned a colonel in the British army.

Red Jacket was a Seneca orator whose speeches are still
often quoted. Red Jacket hated all white men, but he fought
well for the English and was given a red uniform coat by
them. After the Revolution, he became a staunch friend of
George Washington whom he admired because of his fair
treatment of the Iroquois. Washington gave him a silver
medal which he wore constantly, although he remained hostile to all things of the white man until he died. Red Jacket
fought for this country in several important battles in the
War of 1812.

Skenandoah, an Oneida, was as loyal to the Americans as
the others were to England. He warned the settlers of ap-
proaching English invasions many times and he fought for
the Americans in all of the border conflicts along the Mohawk
River. Through his scouts, he was able to secure valuable
information about English plans and troop movements.

After the Revolution, a new religious teacher appeared
among the Six Nations, destined to become one of the greatest of Indian prophets. This was Handsome Lake, a Seneca,
who revived much of the teachings of Dekanawida and Hay-

enwaten. There are followers of Handsome Lake among the present-day Iroquois and they meet each fall to listen to his doctrines and to renew their faith.

During the Civil War, Ely S. Parker, a Seneca, was a civil engineer and a distinguished officer in the Union Army. General Parker was an aide to General Ulysses S. Grant, and it was he who copied out the articles of capitulation for General Robert E. Lee to sign. It was Parker, too, who suggested that the Southerners be allowed to keep their horses after the war so that they could be used in the rebuilding of the South.

Ely Parker was appointed Commissioner of Indian Affairs by Grant when Grant became president. He was the first Indian to hold this office. His nephew, Arthur, was a noted ethnologist and for many years the director of the Rochester Museum of Arts and Science.

E. Pauline Johnson, a Mohawk, was one of Canada's most famous poets. Dr. L. Rosa Minoka Hill, another Mohawk, was one of the first Indian women physicians. Dr. Lucille Johnson Marsh, a Tuscarora, was a long-term employee of the U.S. Public Health Service. Her father, Dr. Philip Johnson, was a Tuscarora chief.

Dr. Gilbert S. Monture, a Mohawk, was a world-famous mineral economist, who has undertaken highly important scientific missions for the Canadian government and the United Nations. Another noted scientist is Arnold Anderson, who was brought up on the Mohawk reserve in Canada. He was one of the key members of the team that undertook the development of atomic energy in World War II. He collaborated with Professor Albert Einstein and, at the conclusion of the war, was cited by the United States government for his valuable services.

Two other Iroquois Indians have held the post of Commissioner of Indian Affairs in recent times. Robert L. Bennett, an Oneida from Wisconsin, was the only individual to come up through the ranks of the Bureau of Indian Affairs to serve in this position. He was in office from 1963 to 1969, stepping out with the change in administration.

Louis R. Bruce, a Mohawk-Sioux from New York State, was appointed by President Richard M. Nixon, and remained in office until 1972. During his administration there was considerable movement in the way of Indian self-determination, with a number of tribes taking over the responsibility for their educational programs. Mr. Bruce at one time was New York State Director of Indians under the National Youth Administration. He is the owner and operator of a large dairy farm in New York. In 1949, he wrote an article on "What America Means to Me," which was published in *American Magazine* and reprinted in other publications around the world.

Of the Wappinger tribes, the Manhattans sold Manhattan Island to the Dutch for eighty guilders or twenty-four dollars worth of trinkets and beads. They had several small villages on the island used only for hunting bases. Their principal village was at Yonkers, New York.

When Henry Hudson sailed down the Hudson River in 1609, the Manhattans went out in two canoes to attack him. This was the first contact the regional tribes had with the white man. Later, the Manhattans sold off all their lands to the Dutch and vanished from sight.

David Nimham was a Wappinger chief who was noted for his activities to recover for his tribe the lands lying along the eastern shore of the Hudson River that had been taken by the English. He was made a chief, or sachem, in 1740, and in spite of his feelings against the English, he entered their service with most of his fighting men in 1755 to fight against the French under Sir William Johnson. In 1762 he, with a few Mohegan chiefs, went to England to pursue the matter of tribal land claims. The claims were brought into court, but with the outbreak of the American Revolution, they were shunted aside.

In the Revolution, Chief Nimham fought with the Americans. With seventeen Stockbridge Indians, he put up a desperate resistance against the British Legion Dragoons in the Battle of Kingsbridge. Nimham wounded Simcoe, the British commander, but was killed by Simcoe's orderly. The Stockbridge Indians were also killed, losing out to superior numbers. Chief Nimham and his Stockbridge warriors are buried where they fell, in a plot of land in Van Cortlandt Park called Indian Field. There is a monument on the site erected to the memory of the brave Stockbridges and their leader, David Nimham.

The Shinnecocks were one of the largest and most important of the Long Island tribes. In 1640, their chief, Nowdemoah, met a sloopload of colonists from Massachusetts and sold them six square miles of land on the island.

There are descendants of the Shinnecocks living on the Oneida Reservation in Wisconsin and a small number of mixed-bloods occupy a reservation near Southampton, Long Island, which they claim was the first to be established. This shore land is some of the most valuable real estate in the country with an estimated value of $45 million.

The Canarsee sold the land comprising the city of Brooklyn to the Dutch. By 1800, the last member of the tribe had died.

The Dutch governors bought the land from the Indians and distributed it among their people, while the English as individuals bought directly from the Indians. But the Indians did not understand that they were selling land. They considered these purchases only agreements of joint occupation and they became hostile when they were ordered away from what they considered their own. It was out of this that the term "Indian giver" arose—a term that is most unjust to the

Indian people, who always gave most generously and without protest. They were justified in their animosity over the land "sales," for they were taken advantage of through misunderstanding.

Those tribes, already decimated by warfare among themselves, now fought courageously against the Dutch until about 1670. Those that survived rapidly disappeared with the first touch of civilization and the introduction of new diseases and unheard-of vices. A very few mixed-blood Montauks, Poosepatucks, Setaukets, and Matinecocks still live near their old homes and, with the Shinnecocks, are the only reminders of the original occupants of Long Island.

The Munsee were a principal tribe of the Delaware. They were deprived of most of their lands by the famous and infamous "Walking Purchase." The Indians had agreed to sell a tract of land that could be walked around in a day. Instead of walking, the purchasers ran, thus acquiring many more acres of land than was bargained for. By 1740, the Munsees began to move west. After several removals, they merged with other remnant groups. The largest number of them now live on the Stockbridge Reservation in Wisconsin.

TRIBES OF NEW YORK STATE

Iroquois Confederacy

Cayuga ("at the place where the locusts were taken out")	Shores of Cayuga Lake
Mohawk ("man eaters")	From eastern New York north to the St. Lawrence River, west nearly to Utica, south nearly to Pennsylvania
Oneida ("people of the stone")	Oneida county
Onondaga ("people of the hill")	Onondaga county
Seneca ("at the standing stone")	From Seneca Lake to Geneva River
Tuscarora ("hemp gatherers")	Madison county

Wappinger Confederacy

Kitchawank ("at the great mountain")	Along Hudson River from mouth of Croton River
Manhattan ("the hill island")	Manhattan Island
Sintsink ("at the small stone")	Around Ossining
Wappinger ("easterners")	Near Poughkeepsie
Wecquaesgeet ("end of the marsh")	Westchester county

Delaware Confederacy

Munsee ("at the place where stones are gathered together")	West bank of Hudson River and headwaters of Delaware River, New Jersey, Pennsylvania

Tribes of Long Island

(There were thirteen main groups, all Algonquian, some of which had subdivisions.)

Canarsee ("the fenced place")	Kings county, Jamaica, lower Manhattan Island
Corchaug ("the greatest or principal place")	Northeast end of island
Manhasset ("island neighborhood")	Shelter and Ram Islands
Massapequa ("great water land")	From Fort Neck to Islip and inland to center of island

Matinecock ("at the hilly land")

Merrick ("at the barren land")

Montauk ("at the fort")

Nesaquake ("the clay or mud country")

Patchogue (Poosepatuck) ("a turning place")

Rockaway ("sandy land")

Secatogue ("black or dark colored land")

Setauket ("land at the south end of a river")

Shinnecock ("at the level land")

Middle of island to north shore from Newton and Flushing to Nissequogue River

Center of island to north shore between Rockville Centre and Fort Neck

Eastern two-thirds of island

Across center of island to north shore between Nissequogue River to Stony Brook

Center of island to south shore between Patchogue and Canoe Place

Diagonal strip from Long Island City to Far Rockaway

Between south shore and center of island from Islip to Patchogue

Between north shore and middle of island from Stony Brook to Wading River

Between Atlantic Ocean and Peconic Bay from Canoe Place to Easthampton

Miscellaneous Tribes

Mahican ("wolf")

Erie ("long-tailed" or "puma people")

Both sides of Hudson River

Along Lake Erie into Pennsylvania

Major Linguistic Stocks
Iroquoian
Algonquian

INDIAN RESERVATIONS IN NEW YORK STATE

Allegany Reservation (Seneca, Cayuga, Onondaga)	Erie county
Cattaraugus Reservation (Seneca, Cayuga, Onondaga)	Cattaraugus county
Tonawanda Reservation (Seneca)	Erie and Genesee counties
Tuscarora Reservation (Tuscarora)	Niagara county
St. Regis Reservation (Mohawk)	St. Lawrence and Franklin counties (extends into Canada)
Onondaga Reservation (Onondaga, Oneida, Cayuga)	Onondaga county

Non-reservation Communities

Montauk	Long Island
Poosepatucks	Long Island
Setaukets	Long Island
Matinecocks	Long Island
Shinnecock	Long Island

Indians of the Mid-Atlantic States

The Delaware Confederacy was the most important of the Algonquian groups in the East. The name Delaware was given to them by the colonists because they occupied the entire basin of the Delaware River. They called themselves the Lenni Lenape, or "real men." Among the Algonquians, they claimed to be the oldest of the tribes, and were referred to as "grandfather," a term of great respect.

Their early contacts with the whites were with William Penn and his Quakers with whom they remained at peace as long as Penn lived—this in spite of the "Walking Purchase," which bilked them of many acres of lands.

It is difficult to assess the number of Delaware people. In New Jersey alone, there were 5,000 when the colonists arrived. Two hundred years later only eighty-five remained. Hostilities with the whites did not take place on Jersey soil, however, until some Indians participated in an attack which was followed by other depredations.

A conference was then called and the Indians were given opportunity to state their grievances. They complained that the whites used large deer traps which depleted the deer supply needed for their food and clothing. Also, that Indians were punished for acts that the white men committed freely without punishment; that they were given "fire water," which destroyed their young men and lost them their homes; and that they were put in prison when they were in debt, although it was difficult to collect money owing to them.

The state legislature moved to limit the size of the traps and established fines against those found giving or selling rum to the Indians. It also purchased 3,000 acres of land to establish an Indian reservation (1758).

Those Delawares living north of the Raritan River sold their rights in New Jersey and moved to western Pennsylvania. The rest of the tribe agreed to live on the reservation, the treaty for which was consummated with Chief Tedyuscung and confirmed with the presentation of a wampum belt showing an Indian and a white man clasping hands.

At first, the reservation was called Brotherton. Then it became known as Indian Mills because some of the Indians owned and operated grist mills. Others worked in nearby foundries and glass works, while the rest sank into despondency and abject poverty.

The effects of civilization took the usual toll of this once proud and mighty people. The ravages of disease and alcohol worsened instead of bettered, and it was almost impossible to control the trade in strong drink. Those who were accustomed to a free life could not plow fields and fell trees. It was hard to have to embrace new ways and the strange religion which the missionaries pressed upon them. Under the influence of the Moravians, however, many of the Delawares became devout Christians.

Forty years went by and then the Mohegan Indians began to send persistent appeals to the "grandfather people," begging them to join them and "spread their mats by the Mohegan fireplace in New York." Signing themselves "grandchildren," the Mohegans invited their "grandfather to eat with his grandchildren out of one dish and with one spoon."

The few Delawares harkened to this plea and decided to go. The governor of New Jersey was petitioned to sell their land, and part of the money financed the journey while the rest was invested in stocks. Twelve rented wagons were loaded with the scanty belongings—a few sticks of furniture, relics dear to them, and the old and the sick. Those who could walk marched behind the wagons to the music of violins.

One of the tribe remained behind. This was Indian Ann Roberts, daughter of Chief Tamar. She lived to be over one hundred and left ninety-one descendants, some of whom still lived in the Trenton area in 1958 and were present at observances marking the 200th anniversary of the reservation.

In 1822, the Delawares again petitioned New Jersey. They wished to move with their friends, the Mohegans, from New York to the vicinity of Green Bay, Wisconsin, where some live today. They asked for the transfer of their stocks and pointed out that they had not received compensation for their hunting and fishing rights when they surrendered their title to the New Jersey lands at the time the reservation was founded.

Aged Wilted Grass, trembly yet standing with dignity, appeared before the legislature and pleaded for justice. "I am old and weak and poor and therefore a fit representative of my people," he said. "We have ever looked up to the leaders of the United States and to those in this state as our fathers, protectors, and friends. We humbly beg that you will look upon us with that eye of pity as we have reason to think our poor, untutored fathers looked upon yours when they first arrived upon our then extensive but uncultivated dominion and sold them their lands in many instances for trifles in comparison as light as air."

He could also have reminded them that the Lenni Lenape had not the slightest concept of individual ownership of property. What they thought they had given in exchange for gifts was merely the right to hunt and fish on their land. The bank stocks were transferred to the Indians but it was not until some years later that $2,000 was authorized as payment for the hunting and fishing rights.

Chief Tedyuscung, who negotiated the treaty for the New Jersey reservation, was a Munsee. His name meant "one who makes the earth tremble," and he did not become a chief until he was fifty years old. The colonists called him "Honest John." Tedyuscung played an important part in colonial history. He was influential in wresting the Ohio country from the French and in winning the friendship of hostile tribes of the frontier. There is a statue honoring him in Fairmount Park, Philadelphia.

Chief Tamenend was another of the early Delaware chiefs, and perhaps one of the greatest. He was venerated by all and endowed with wisdom, virtue, prudence, charity, and other good and noble qualities in high degree. During the Revolution, Tamenend became known to his enthusiastic admirers as St. Tammany, the patron saint of America, and his feast day was celebrated on the first of May. Tammany societies were organized in a number of cities as patriotic and charitable groups devoted to securing and broadening the foundations of the new young republic. Most of the members had been Revolutionary soldiers. In New York City, the Tammany Society became the dominating factor in the Democratic politics of the city, and everything was referred to "Tammany Hall." Though no longer a political force, the name of Tammany Hall is still in use in Democratic circles.

The Delawares of Pennsylvania and Delaware, who were known as the "praying Indians," removed to Ohio. One of their towns was destroyed and the people massacred by settlers angered by Indian depredations that had taken place on the Pennsylvania frontier, but in which the Delawares had no part. Soon after this, they were forced to cede all of their lands east of the Mississippi and go to the country in the fork of the Kansas and Missouri rivers. By now, the Delawares were thoroughly discouraged and turned against all missionaries and anything Christian. A year before this took place, another great Delaware was born, destined to lead and sustain them in this time of great distress.

Charles Journeycake was the son of a Christian convert who refused to give up her religion. In spite of the people's displeasure, she taught it to her son on the long trail to the West. Charles was the first of the tribe to be baptized and converted west of the Mississippi, and the first Protestant baptized in the state of Kansas. He began to preach soon after his conversion and was able to bring many of the Indians back to the Christian faith in which he never wavered. He was ordained as a minister but not until many years after his conversion by his own desire.

When he was quite a young man, he began to develop as one of the greatest of Indian statesmen. He was chosen principal chief of the tribe—the last to have this title.

Again the Delawares were forced to move, this time to Indian Territory, now the state of Oklahoma. They were joined by some of the Delawares still living in Wisconsin. Charles wrote a constitution for the tribe which was a masterpiece and which contained well-defined laws for the protection of the freedom and rights of the people.

Soon after various eastern tribes were removed to Oklahoma, the Creek Tribal Council granted 160 acres of Creek lands on which a school would be built for Christian Indian students. This was to become Bacone College, the oldest continuous institution of higher learning in the state and still educating young Indian people. Bacone has many distinguished graduates.

Charles Journeycake was one of those who helped to establish the college and on the cornerstone of the chapel these famous words of his are inscribed. They are a lesson to all in strength and fortitude and shaming to those who treated the Delawares so outrageously.

"We have been broken up and moved six times. We have been despoiled of our property. We thought when we moved across the Missouri River and paid for our homes in Kansas we were safe, but in a few years the white man wanted our country. We had good farms, built comfortable houses and big barns. We had schools for our children and churches where we listened to the same gospel the white man listened to. The white man came into our country from Missouri and drove our cattle and our horses away and if our people followed them, they were killed. We try to forget these things, but we would not forget that the white man brought to us the blessed gospel of Christ, the Christian's hope. This more than pays for all that we have suffered."

In 1964, Delaware Indians living in Oklahoma were invited to take part in the New Jersey Tercentennial and did so. The Tribal Council president said that "they were glad and honored to have a place in the program and to know that they were not forgotten."

In Pennsylvania—aside from the Delawares—the Senecas, Conestogas, and Susquehannas were all important tribes.

The Conestogas were first met by Captain John Smith in 1608. They were conquered by the Iroquois in 1675 and moved to Maryland where they settled along the Potomac and became closely allied with the Swedish and Dutch settlers and the Maryland English. The Iroquois continued to fight relentlessly against them and they dwindled from a population of 3,000 to 550 people. Some finally moved to New York and settled among the Oneidas, and the remaining twenty were massacred by settlers who were inflamed by acts of Indian warfare on the frontier.

The Susquehannas are described as being a very tall people—almost giants. They lived in palisaded towns, were great warriors, and went about without clothing, but they painted their faces red, green, or white, sometimes with black stripes. To them were attributed qualities of nobility and heroism far beyond other tribes.

Cornplanter was a principal chief of the Senecas during the Revolution. His village extended for a mile along the banks of the Allegheny River. He fought against the Americans in the war, but later firmly supported them. He constantly tried to bring about understanding between Indians and whites and he was influential in negotiating a number of treaties.

Cornplanter was noted for his courage, talent, eloquence, and sobriety, and for his love for his tribe and race. He devoted all of his energy and time, and all that he had, to the welfare of his people, as a chief was required to do.

In 1789, the Pennsylvania General Assembly granted him fifteen hundred acres of land, which included the land belonging to his village. At Cornplanter's request, a mission school was opened on his grant in which eleven Indian boys and several white children were enrolled. When Chief Cornplanter died, a monument was erected at his grave by the state of Pennsylvania, which is said to be the first ever erected to an Indian by a public body.

The Cornplanter Reservation was the scene of a bitter fight over land taken for the construction of Kinzua Dam in 1964. These were lands promised to the Indians by George Washington. There was a nationwide protest over the violation of the treaty with the Senecas and over the removal of Seneca families to make way for the water backup from the dam. The Senecas took matters into court in a losing battle. They finally agreed to relinquish the land for a settlement of nearly $3 million and another $12 million for a development program. They gave up about one-third of their land.

One of the most important Indians in early America was Chief Shikellamy, an Oneida, who is described as the most picturesque and historic Indian to live in Philadelphia. Shikellamy was sent by the Iroquois to act as their ambassador and protector of their interests in the Susquehanna Valley. He conducted many important missions between the Pennsylvania governors and the Iroquois council.

A man of great dignity and prudence, Shikellamy was markedly kind to all white people at all times. In 1745, he was made vice regent over those tribes who were tributary to the Iroquois in the valley. He handled all important and intricate tasks assigned to him with the skill of a diplomat, and helped to settle many disputes. It is said that he took part at the negotiation of all treaties in which the Iroquois were interested in colonial times. He made so many important contributions that it would be difficult to list them all. A statue memorializes Shikellamy in Conrad Weiser Memorial Park and a monument marks his gravesite in Sunbury, Pennsylvania.

TRIBES OF THE MID-ATLANTIC STATES

(New Jersey, Delaware, Maryland, Pennsylvania)

Delaware Confederacy
Delaware (Lenni Lenape, "real men")
Munsee ("at the place where stones are gathered together")
Unalachtigo
Unami

Entire basin of Delaware River in eastern Pennsylvania, southeast New York, most of New Jersey and Delaware

Nanticoke Confederacy
Arseek
Conoy
Cuscarawaoc
Nanse
Nanticoke ("tidewater people")
Ozinies·
Sarapinagh

Maryland

Miscellaneous Tribes

Acquintanacsuak	Maryland
Atquanachuke	New Jersey
Chapticon	Maryland
Choptank	Maryland
Conestoga ("place of the inverted pole")	Pennsylvania
Erie	Pennsylvania
Hackensack	New Jersey
Kahansuk	New Jersey
Nacotchtank	Maryland
Piscataway	District of Columbia
Raritan	New Jersey
Shawnee ("southerners")	Pennsylvania
Susquehanna	Pennsylvania

Major Linguistic Stocks
Algonquian
Iroquoian

INDIAN RESERVATIONS IN THE MID-ATLANTIC STATES

No reservations *

Non-reservation Communities

NEW JERSEY
    Mixed tribes   Essex county

DELAWARE
    Nanticoke   Sussex county
    Mixed tribes   Kent and Sussex counties

MARYLAND
    Nanticoke   Frederick and Washington
                                       counties
    Wesort   Charles   and   Prince
                                         Georges counties

PENNSYLVANIA
    Cherokee   Dauphin county
    Mixed tribes   Bradford   and   Dauphin
                                       counties

---

* The Cornplanter Reservation (Seneca) in Warren county, Pennsylvania, is no longer occupied. This was not a tribal reservation, but was the grant land given to Cornplanter and his followers by the United States government. The Indians were removed when the land was taken for the construction of Kinzua Dam.

Indians of the South Atlantic Coast

The South Atlantic area was one of the most populated the country. Virginia and South Carolina, especially, were the homes of many tribes, and Florida, too, shared in large numbers.

Long before the English ships brought their cargoes of settlers, the Spaniards were traveling around Florida and it was near this area that Columbus first anchored his three small vessels with their crew of eighty-eight men. Columbus never reached the mainland of North America and so knew nothing of the thousands of Indian people already living there. The Indian people whom he did meet were the Caribs, and he found them a gentle and generous people.

In 1570, the Spaniards established a Jesuit mission in Virginia, but this was short-lived. There were no other whites in Virginia until the arrival of the Jamestown colonists in 1607.

Although we think most often of the Pilgrims and the Indians, it was actually the Powhatans who first met up with the English settlers and who held the destiny of the newcomers in their hands.

The Powhatan Confederacy of the Algonquian family was the strongest group in Virginia. It was comprised of some thirty tribes with some 200 villages. The chief of the Confederacy was Wahonsonacock, whom the English called Powhatan. He had numerous wives and children, of whom Pocahontas was his favorite. She is one of the most famous women in history.

The story of Captain John Smith and of how he was saved from death by Pocahontas is an American classic and found in every history book. But Pocahontas did more than save Smith. She also saved the colony from starvation and attack —not once, but several times. She made it possible for the struggling little group to survive and the grateful settlers said that she, "next to God, was the instrument to preserve the colony from death, famine and utter confusion." This saying is inscribed on the statue which memorializes the young Indian maiden at Jamestown.

Although Powhatan was disposed to be friendly to the English, his brother, Opechancanough, hated them and tried to turn Powhatan against them. It was necessary to secure Powhatan's friendship and every effort was made to do so. Captain Smith tried to bring Powhatan to Jamestown to be honored in a coronation ceremony, but the chief refused to leave his village. He said that he was already a king and would not go to anybody except by his own desire.

Smith then arranged for the ceremony to be held under a great tree on the riverbank near Powhatan's village. To this spot were brought gifts for Powhatan—a set of bedroom and other furniture, and a pitcher and a basin. Powhatan accepted the gift of a scarlet cape, but he would not kneel to be crowned, and finally he was forced to do so by Smith's men. When the crown was in place, a ceremonial salute was fired which frightened Powhatan, who tried to run away. When he was calmed at last, he asked that his old moccasins and his deerskin cloak be taken to his new brother, King James. The furniture was left under the great tree. The cloak may be seen in the British Museum in London.

Relations were to become increasingly strained with the Indians and, in spite of their gratitude, the colonists were not adverse to seizing Pocahontas and holding her in Jamestown as a hostage. She lived in the home of a minister and was converted to Christianity, baptized, and given the name of Rebecca. She was trained in the ways of English life and married John Rolfe, a wealthy young colonist.

The wedding was hailed with delight as a bond that would make peace with the Indians certain. Powhatan, however, refused to come to the wedding, although he sent gifts and allowed two of his sons to attend.

After the birth of their son, the Rolfes went to England. There Pocahontas was a great favorite, especially of the Court. She was known as Lady Rebecca or Princess Rebecca. When she was twenty-one, Rolfe arranged to return to Virginia. But Pocahontas, who had been in failing health, was fatally stricken as they waited to board ship at Gravesend. She died speaking words of gladness that her son would live after her. . .

At the time of the marriage of Pocahontas, the Chickahominies who lived the closest to Jamestown made their own peace treaty with the colonists. They lived together in harmony and these Indians taught the English many things about forest ways.

A stipulation of this treaty was that every fighting man, at the beginning of the harvest, would pay the English two bushels of corn as a tribute, receiving in return the same number of hatches. Eight leading men of the tribe were to act as overseers and were to be paid each a red coat, a copper chain, a picture of King James, and the "honor of being his noblemen."

The Chickahominy is the largest tribe living in Virginia today. Their homes are on both sides of the river bearing their name in New Kent and Charles counties. The land is incorporated by the state and the Indians pay taxes, vote, own their land individually, and send their children to public schools. They have their own chief and maintain their integrity as a tribe.

Only two tribes live within the state on reservations. These are the Pamunkey and the Mattaponi. The Pamunkey was the largest tribe of the Powhatan Confederacy. In a treaty made with the two, it was required that twenty beaver skins were to be brought to the governor in acknowledgment that they held their lands by the grace of the King of England. When the beaver became extinct, the Pamunkey were required to make a tribute of game, skins, or fish. This treaty is still being observed by the Indians, of their own volition, and the annual gifts are brought to the governor at Thanksgiving.

The Indians pay no taxes on their land and are governed by a chief and a council elected by Indian ritual every four years. For the two reservations, the state provides dental services and maintains the entering roads. It pays tuition for Indians in public schools, but not beyond high school.

The Cherokees, who occupied a major portion of the South, were an extremely powerful tribe and their sad story would fill many pages. Of the Iroquois family, the Cherokees sided against the Americans in the Revolution. At that time, Nancy Ward was a Cherokee woman of great influence. She had the title of "Beloved Woman," which meant that she was head of the Woman's Council and as such could veto any order given by the chief and headmen for the death of a prisoner. This was customary among many of the eastern tribes, for women did not occupy the menial place usually attributed to them. In the Iroquoian tribes, especially, they had much power and prestige.

Nancy, like Pocahontas, saved the lives of captives and befriended the American colonists, even though her people were loyal to the English. As a young woman, she had been a warrior woman and had fought as bravely as any man alongside her husband. With his death, she settled down to ways of peace. She persuaded her people to take up dairying and owned the first cow among them. She also interested them in the cattle industry and in developing intensive farming.

The Americans inflicted terrible punishment on the Cheokees during the war, for in order to break the hold of England, they must also break the strength of the Indian allies. At the war's end, the Cherokees were the first tribe to pledge allegiance to the United States and to sign a treaty with the government.

For a time, all went well. Educational and missionary work began and it was not long before the people had advanced well on the road of progress. They had their own farms, a weaving industry, and their own government patterned after that of the United States.

When Sequoyah created the Cherokee alphabet, they were able to read and write in their own language, to establish their own schools, and their own newspaper published in Cherokee. Many owned large tracts of land and kept Negro slaves to cultivate them. They were as wealthy as the plantation owners surrounding them and as highly cultured. Indian customs and ways rapidly disappeared.

As the years went by, settlers began to crowd in on the Indians and to press for their removal. The government established a policy that all Indians were to be moved west of the Mississippi to land which was set aside for them "forever" as Indian Territory. The government added the weight of its pressure to that of the settlers. Some of the people thought it best to go and drifted away to Arkansas. Others said they would defend their homes with their lives.

With the discovery of gold in Georgia, the hue and cry against the Indians broke loose and with that happening, the Cherokees were doomed. Their homes and properties were seized and they were rounded up and forced to march away, leaving everything behind them. That march, known as the "Trail of Tears," was made in the bitter winter months and more than one-fourth of the people died and were buried along the way. The rest tried to begin over again in the new country, were once more devastated by the Civil War and once more re-established themselves. Then the land that was to be theirs "forever" was taken away to become part of the state of Oklahoma.

In the troublesome times of the removal and before, there were a number of great leaders, but none so great as John Ross. Ross was principal chief of the Cherokee Nation and the main architect of the governmental constitution. He fought for his people with great courage and brilliance.

The Cherokee Reservation in North Carolina is the largest reservation in the East. It is comprised of 56,000 acres and is governed by an elected chief and a twelve-member council. The Cherokees living there are descendants of those who defied the soldiers and fled to the hills when the people were being gathered up and placed in a stockade prior to removal. They were allowed to remain when Tsali gave his life in forfeit so that his people might keep their beloved hill country. This story is dramatized in the beautiful pageant, "Unto These Hills," which is given nightly on the reservation during the summer months.

The Cherokee Reservation is often pointed to as a model of progress. The Indians have seven civic clubs, own and operate their own fleet of school buses, a luxury motel—the first to be opened on any reservation—and three industrial

1. An Iroquois long house. Such dwellings, made of saplings and bark, housed as many as twenty families. There were no windows, but light entered through the doors and smoke holes.

2. Builders of the ancient cliff dwellings in the canyons and on the mesas of the Southwest were probably ancestors of the present-day Pueblo Indians. These communal dwellings were difficult of access and easily defended. Crops were raised in the valleys below. This is Montezuma Castle near Prescott, Arizona, now a national monument. It is believed to have been built in 1100 A.D., is five stories high and 46 feet from cliff base.

3. The Pamunkey and Mattaponi tribes of Virginia voluntarily observe a treaty of 1677 by presenting a tribute of game, skins, or fish each year to the governor at Thanksgiving time. Chief Curtis Custalow of the Mattaponi offers their gifts.

4. Statue representing Chief Tedyuskung of the Munsee tribe

5. *Above:* Cherokee basket of plaited river cane. Height, thirteen inches.

6. *Left:* Lucy George, Cherokee basket maker

7. Modern motel operated by the Eastern Band of Cherokee Indians is located on the Cherokee Reservation in North Carolina.

8. Seminole woman wearing clothing peculiar only to the Seminoles

9. 10. *Left:* Traditional chickee of Seminole Indians in Florida. *Below:* Modernized chickee on Miccosukee Reservation in Florida.

11. Seminole Indians on Big Cypress Reservation in traditional dress

12. 13. Dancing was important to all tribes, as physical exercise but also because of the many rituals based on dancing. *Left:* Choctaw boy dancing in modern costume. *Right:* Seminole participating in American Indian Festival of Arts.

14. Serpent Mound in Ohio, one of the largest and finest examples of an effigy mound, built by Indians thousands of years ago.

15. Artifacts from Mound Builders' tombs in Lewiston, Illinois

16. Restored Mandan earth lodge at Fort Lincoln state park in North Dakota. The Mandans had permanent villages. Often favorite dogs and horses were kept inside the dome-shaped lodges.

17. A Potawatomi woman weaves a hamper similar to the one at left which she recently completed.

18. 19. *Left:* Sauk and Fox women, showing distinctive ribbonwork costumes of Woodland tribes. *Right:* Winnebago woman and child.

20. 21. Two types of Chippewa homes at Mille Lacs, Minnesota.
Above: A "maple sugar" wigwam in which the poles are very
heavy in order to support maple sugar pots. In fall leaves are
piled around the base for warmth. *Below:* A wigwam made of
saplings driven into the ground, bound together at the top, and
covered with birchbark.

22. Catching the ripe grain heads with one stick, this elderly Chippewa wild rice harvester thrashes them with another so that the grain will fall into his boat.

23. A Chippewa at Little Rice Lake near Tower, Minnesota, with his hand-made birchbark canoe for harvesting wild rice.

24. Chippewa woman preparing corn for winter drying. The ears are bundled together with buckskin thongs and hung to dry on log rafters. Nett Lake Reservation, Minnesota.

25. At the wild rice camp in Minnesota a Chippewa family parches rice over a log fire while the children play near a temporary wigwam built in the traditional fashion to shelter harvesters.

26. Chippewa girl in full dress

27. 28. *Below:* Chippewa workers at machine shop at Lac du Flambeau, Wisconsin, and workers of Red Cliff Band of Chippewa at tribally-operated garment shop on their reservation.

29. 30. *Above:* Iowa Indians hold a pow-wow at Whitecloud, Kansas. *Below:* Kiowa "Black Leggins" Warrior Society dance.

31. 32. *Above:* Crow Indians in Plains regalia. Barney Old Coyote (right) and his son. *Below:* A typical Plains tipi.

33. Bark house of the Kansa tribe

34. Kickapoo bark house, photographed, Indian Territory, 1875

35. Plains Indian war dancers

36. Five-year-old Mesquakie (Fox) dancer

37. *Right:* Salish woman of Montana wearing dress with hand-beaded yoke.

38. *Below:* Salish Indian feast during ceremonial celebration on the Flathead Reservation in Montana.

39. 40. *Left:* Sioux breastplate of porcupine quills on rawhide. *Right:* Kiowa necklace of glass beads.

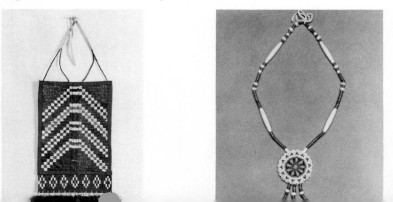

plants employing Indian labor. A craft shop sells Cherokee-made crafts, among them the fine woodcarvings made by Cherokee artisans, and handmade furniture.

One of the famous woodcarvers is Amanda Crowe, a young woman who is known the country over for her lifelike animals made from the beautiful native woods. As a schoolgirl, Amanda was never without a pocketknife and a piece of wood, and her animals were wanted even then. When she was orphaned, she went to live with friends in Chicago where she attended school and studied art. She won a number of scholarships, including a fellowship for study in Mexico, and carved her way through college, paying for her tuition with her work.

As soon as she could, she returned to the reservation as a teacher of woodcarving, developing this skill, which is natural to the Cherokee, into an art. Amanda continues to win prizes, but she is proudest of those won by her students. Cherokee woodcarving is now an important source of revenue, with the finer pieces quickly purchased as soon as they are placed on view.

An outstanding modern-day leader is Jarrett Blythe, who is one of the most revered men on the Cherokee Reservation. Mr. Blythe has spent all of his life among his people. He comes from a family noted as leaders and he served as chief of the tribe for twenty-four years, longer than any other person. He was first elected to this office in 1931.

Jarrett Blythe was directly responsible for much of the progress on the reservation and many of the acts of his administration are living memorials to his concern and compassion for others. He was a founder of the Cherokee Historical Society, and initiated the start of the historical drama, "Unto These Hills," and the construction of the Boundary Tree Inn motor court. He was also instrumental in the establishment of the replica of an early Cherokee village, which is a reservation tourist attraction.

Without children of his own, he and his wife cared for many neglected waifs, giving them a home and a start in life. So that young people could get started in business, he initiated a tribal loan fund, and he has made gifts of his own property to some who wanted to farm.

The marks of his administrations as chief are the milestones set up along the way for the benefit of his people. In recognition of his devoted life and outstanding accomplishments, he was awarded the Indian Achievement Award in 1956. Now an "elder statesman," he is held in the greatest affection and respect by members of the tribe who still turn to him for wise counsel.

The Lumbee Indians living in North Carolina along the Lumber River, from which they take their name, are thought to be the descendants of the lost colony of Roanoke and the Croatan tribe. Their past is cloaked in mystery and there is little of Indian culture among them. Brantley Blue, a Lumbee, heads the U.S. Indian Claims Commission, which has the responsibility for determining the awards made in the settlement of Indian land claims.

Some thirty tribes once lived in South Carolina and twenty-three of them made up the Catawba Nation. Continually friendly to the English, the Catawba, a Siouan group, sided with them in the French and Indian War and in the Revolution. Originally numbering around 6,000, they dwindled under the constant warfare carried on with other tribes and the attacks made upon them. Several smallpox epidemics reduced them even further and one such epidemic destroyed more than half the tribe. By the end of the eighteenth century they were only a remnant people.

In 1763, a treaty with England allocated to them 144,000 acres of land in York and Lancaster counties, a mere fragment of their original holdings. By 1820, most of this land was leased to whites for a few thousand dollars. Later, it was sold to the state except for a single square mile where a small group of Catawbas lived in poverty.

In 1943, they were in such misery that the state of South Carolina gave them funds for land and other purposes and the Indians were declared citizens of the state. The acquired land was divided among individuals, and homesites and small gardens were established. A portion of the land was reserved for timber growth and a cattle range. Federal aid assisted with a development program and by 1954 it was claimed that the Catawba had made more progress in the ten-year period than any other tribe in the United States. Independent of spirit, the tribe severed its ties to the federal government as soon as it could and declined further special services.

A principal chief of the Catawbas was King Hagler, a man of sterling character who was respected by the whites and loved by his people. He was just in all of his dealings and was a father to the tribe, striving in every way to be of help to them. This was ever the tradition of the great chiefs.

Hagler was inclined to ways of peace, but he offered his services to South Carolina when war broke out with the Cherokees and was active in some of the most severe battles. While still in the prime of life, he was ambushed and slain by a party of Shawnees.

The Shawnees were also a leading tribe of the area, roving into Kentucky and Tennessee. There was scarcely a tribe in the East that moved as much as they did, and they moved into Pennsylvania and finally to Ohio in early times.

Of the early Florida tribes, the Calusa occupied much of the southern coast. Their history, as we know it, begins with Ponce de Leon whom they boldly attacked in a fleet of eighty canoes as he was about to land on Florida soil. De Leon was forced to withdraw after an all-day fight.

From their fifty villages, the Calusa made a business of attacking Spanish vessels in the Florida Keys and they were noted for the golden wealth they accumulated from wrecked vessels. In time, they became pirates, plundering without mercy all ships unfortunate enough to come to grief in their neighborhood.

They carried on a regular trade with Havana, bartering fish, skins, and amber, and were much under the influence of Spain. When Florida was transferred to England by Spain, the Calusa were driven from the mainland by the Creeks and other English allies, and relocated to the Keys. Later, the last eighty families removed to Havana and were lost sight of.

The Seminoles were emigrants from the Creeks in Georgia and some other tribes living north of Florida, leaving their homes because of the clash between Spanish and English politics. These Indians merged together and with other Florida groups, and became known as the Seminoles, or "runaways." By then, most of the Florida tribes had been killed off or sold into slavery in Cuba by the Spaniards.

The Seminoles were formed as a tribe about the time of the American Revolution. They spread over northern Florida and, because their land was rich and fertile, they grew prosperous. They carried on an extensive trade with the Spaniards for coffee, sugar, and tobacco.

The Americans, now colonizing along the Georgia-Florida border, did not forgive the Indians for aiding the English in the war and were further irritated by their harboring of Negro runaway slaves. A proud people, the Seminoles would never be slaves and they were quite willing to help those who wanted to escape. The Negroes lived among them like tenant farmers and some even became tribal leaders.

There were many clashes with the Americans. Finally, in

1812, fearing that the English would win their former friends to their cause once more, General Andrew Jackson was sent with troops to make war upon the Seminoles. Villages were burned and plundered, horses and cattle were taken and the people were scattered. Spanish authority was so weakened that Florida was ceded to the United States and Seminole troubles began in earnest.

In 1823, a treaty was drawn up and the Seminoles agreed to give up 52,000,000 acres of land for a 4,000,000-acre reservation in central Florida. All were to live there and were promised that they would live in peace if they abided by United States laws. They were given farm implements, livestock, food rations, and funds for a school, and a yearly payment of $5,000 to the tribe was to continue for twenty years.

The change in the way of life was too sudden and worked great hardship. The land was poor and not suited for farming, although the Seminoles were good farmers. There was little drinking water. The acreage was too small for the large number of people. In a short time, the Indians began to raid nearby settlements for food, for they had none and were barely able to survive.

As with the Cherokees, there was strong pressure for Indian removal and the government tried to make the Indians agree to leave for Indian Territory. Some said they would go, and a new treaty gave them $15,400 in payment for their Florida lands. But most were determined to stay and refused flatly to budge one step. War broke out anew.

The Seminoles had always been fearless warriors. They refused to surrender in battle but fought until they could fight no more. Then they would break ranks and escape into the swamps and woods. In a twinkling they were out of sight.

The Indians fought bitterly and fiercely for nearly eight years. With only 1,500 fighting men, they were driven from place to place by several thousand soldiers who could never quite catch up with them. But at last, they had to give in and the removal to the West took place.

One small band held out and fled into the swamps, where they lived off the land, ready to fight or to run at a moment's notice. Small children were hidden in pits and visited only at night out of fear that the soldiers would find them. No one spoke above a whisper in the villages so shielded by the tall swamp grass that they could not be seen. No trails led through the swamp. Because it was so impossible to reach them, the Indians were allowed to remain, and for many years they lived in the swamps which are called the Everglades.

Here again were new conditions demanding a new lifestyle. Open huts thatched with palm leaves, called *chickees*, were designed for greater comfort in the hot, humid climate, and which blended with the swamp growth.

The Seminoles became a boat people, traveling the swamp in dugout canoes of their own making which were poled through the water. They knew every waterway as well as they had once known the trails on land and they found their way through the jungle growth without difficulty. They left no ruffling of the water behind them to give away the passage of their boats.

They hated the white man for all the suffering caused them, and would make or accept no offers of friendship. They did not welcome visitors and left their villages only when they had to buy food or other necessities at a nearby trading center. They refused to adopt the white man's ways or learn his language. They made do with very little, asking only to be let alone. The swamps were their stronghold and their sanctuary.

Somewhere along the way, these Indians had exchanged their deerskin clothing for long, loose-fitting garments made of cloth obtained from traders. Because of the millions of mites and mosquitoes, they had to keep their bodies covered. It is said that they wore clothing much like the Indians of Peru—certainly, it was clothing that was influenced by the Spaniards.

Then, by some twist of fate, a trader introduced a sewing machine. This was one white man's article that the women accepted with eagerness. In no time, every *chickee* had its small, portable, hand-turned sewing machine and yards and yards of cloth were sewn together in small and intricate patterns from which to make clothing. Calico, gingham, and cotton material was cut into hundreds and hundreds of small pieces and stitched together in strips of delicate and colorful designs. The design strips were then sewn together with bands of colored cloth between them. In one skirt, there might be as many as 5,000 small bits of cloth, all stitched together with the sewing machine in the finest kind of patchwork. The skill with which the tiny pieces were sewn together was incredible and each garment was a work of art. These colorful clothes are still worn by many of the Seminoles today.

Osceola was the most famous of all Seminoles and one of the greatest and most famous of all American Indians. It was he who led the people in the second Seminole War.

"The Seminoles will fight until the last drop of our blood has moistened the dust of our hunting grounds," Osceola said. He was a young man and not a chief, but he was a hero and the Indians followed him without question. It was he who led them into the swamps and who attacked and harassed the soldiers wherever he could find them. Had it not been for the Everglades and Osceola, there would not be a single Seminole alive in Florida today. The soldiers could win few victories against him.

After two years of desperate fighting, Osceola asked to

meet with the Army officers to discuss terms for peace, for the Indians were barely able to continue fighting. He said that they would not leave Florida, but asked to be allowed to continue to live in the swamp. While the party met under a flag of truce, Osceola was seized and with others of his men was imprisoned. Even so, the war went on for several more years.

Those who were with Osceola managed to escape, but he refused to go with them. His spirit broken, he died in prison and was buried with full military honors. Even his enemies spoke of him in the highest terms as a man of gallantry who never harmed women or children and who deserved a better fate. There are more places named for Osceola than for any other one Indian.

Of all Indian tribes, the Seminole is the only one that can say it was never conquered and never signed a peace treaty. The 1,000 or more still living in Florida on three reservations are independent in nature and prefer to keep to themselves. They have never received money from the government and are reluctant to accept any free services available to them through the state in the way of welfare benefits and programs. In 1970, the tribe was awarded more than $12 million for land taken by the military at the time of the Seminole wars.

Now that the children go to public schools, old barriers are breaking down and although older people still live in the traditional *chickees*, modern ranch-style houses have been introduced and a million-dollar land program partly financed by the tribe has developed more than 13,000 acres of improved pasture and farmlands. Sixty-six acres have been set aside for an industrial park, and future plans, in line with the encouragement of tourism, have been made for a forty-unit motel, restaurant, swimming pool, and golf course.

The Indians have a cattle industry and raise a fine strain

of cattle. Stock raising is also a major industry. Both men and women are employed in state conservation projects, and many of the palm leaves used by the churches of the country at Easter are gathered by Seminole workers. Seminole craft work is also an important source of revenue. A large craft shop, the heart of a reproduced Seminole village, offers articles made by both men and women, among them the colorful clothes which make the Seminoles so distinctive.

The Miccosukee, a similar group to the Seminole but speaking a different language, formally organized as a tribe in 1961. Their reservation is a strip of land along the Tamiami Trail, five and a half miles long and 500 feet wide. They also own 76,600 acres on which no one lives and which is held in trust by the state. These people have opened a fine restaurant and a modern community center.

There are no longer any tribal chiefs, but both tribes have organized under a constitution with an elected council and president. In 1968, for the first time in their history, the Seminoles elected a woman—Mrs. Betty Jumper—to head the tribal council. She is the first Seminole to have graduated from high school.

Of the prominent tribes of the South, none was more so than the large and powerful Creek Nation, one of the largest divisions of the Muskhogean family and occupying some fifty towns. They were so-named by the English because of the great number of streams in their territory.

The Creeks sold a considerable amount of their Georgia lands to the English at an early date, Trading posts at Savannah and elsewhere flourished and the Creeks soon began to take on the ways of their English friends.

De Soto came among the Creeks in 1540 but they did not become prominent in history until they were allies of the English and treaty allies of the South Carolina colonists. They were unfriendly to the Spaniards in Florida and bitter enemies of the Cherokees, who were also English allies but who hated the Creeks with equal fervor.

Tomochichi was a Creek chief noted in the early history of Georgia. His village was on the site of the city of Savannah and he was instrumental in bringing about a treaty of alliance between James Oglethorpe and the Georgia colonists and the Creeks of what were called the "lower towns."

With his wife and nephew, Tomochichi accompanied Oglethorpe on a trip to England where a well-known portrait of him was painted. He continued to be helpful to the colonists until his death, when he was probably seventy-five years old, and he was given a public funeral in Savannah. There is a monument to his memory in that city.

Alexander McGillivray was one of the more unusual Creek leaders in colonial times. He was the son of a wealthy Scotch trader who had married the daughter of a Creek chief. He was raised as an Indian until he was fourteen and then was sent to Charleston to be educated. With the outbreak of the Revolution, he returned to his people. As chief, he was an extremely astute leader, of superior ability, and a skilled diplomat. He was courted by both Spain and the United States, and as his fame spread among neighboring tribes they, too, came to him for counsel.

Because of McGillivray's widespread influence, various land organizations and corporations tried to gain him as a stockholder as insurance against Indian attacks. He was largely responsible for the success of the trader, William Panton, who became America's first millionaire, and he himself also became wealthy as a partner of the Panton firm.

Spain appointed McGillivray as a commissioner to the Creeks at a high salary and he was able to block the migration of the Americans into Florida. With a change in the policies of Spain, he was forced to make peace with his former enemies and did so, hoping that he could secure American guns and ammunition to build up a reserve supply.

In 1790, McGillivray, with other chiefs, went to New York City and signed a treaty with Washington's new government. He was obliged to give up some of the Creek lands, but he agreed, with tongue in cheek, to trade with the Americans. He was appointed Indian agent with rank equal to that of a brigadier general, but neither the Americans or the Spaniards honored the treaty so it came to nothing.

While visiting his friend Panton in Pensacola, McGillivray became suddenly ill and died. Since he was a member of that order, he was given a Masonic funeral and buried in the garden of the Panton home in Pensacola while the Creeks wailed in mourning.

Hillis Hadjo, although a Creek, was a leader of the Seminoles in the Florida Indian wars. Seeking help, he went to England where he was royally feted and given a commission as brigadier general in the English army, but no help was forthcoming. The crown prince, who was to become King George IV, gave him a tomahawk mounted in gold and he received many other gifts, among them a diamond-studded snuff box and a fine uniform.

His daughter, Milly Hadjo Francis, whose real name was Malee, became another Pocahontas when she saved the life of Duncan MacKrimmon, a captured American soldier, who was to be executed at the stake. Milly appealed to her father, but since MacKrimmon was a captive of the Seminoles, he said that the Seminoles must decide. She pleaded several times for his life, and finally he was freed after promising to join the tribe. MacKrimmon remained with the Seminoles until they traded him off. Once free, he betrayed Milly's father to General Andrew Jackson. Hillis was captured and hanged as a traitor.

Milly and her family, with other Creeks, were imprisoned in the fort at St. Marks. While there, MacKrimmon asked her to marry him but she declined. She did not save his life for that purpose. At the time, her family was wealthy and owned a large number of slaves. She was a beautiful young girl, and many of the Creek braves were eager to marry her.

Milly went to Indian Territory with the tribe and was discovered, some years later, living in wretched poverty and with several children whom she struggled to support. Major Ethan Allen Hitchcock became interested in her story and convinced the Secretary of War and Congress that her humanitarian act toward MacKrimmon deserved reward. It was decided to give her a Congressional medal and a pension. Several years went by before word of this reached Milly who was dying of tuberculosis. She smiled with delight, but she was buried long before either came to her.

TRIBES OF THE SOUTH ATLANTIC COAST

(Virginia, West Virginia, North Carolina, South Carolina, Georgia, Florida)

Catawba Confederacy   Carolinas, Virginia
Catawba ("divided")
Cheraw
Congaree
Coosa
Eno
Etiwaw
Keyauwee
Nahyesan
Occaneechi
Pedee ("something good")
Santee ("the river is in the middle")
Saponi
Sewee
Shokori
Sissipahaw
Sugeree ("stingy people")
Tutelo
Waccamaw
Wateree
Waxhaw
Winyaw
Woccon
Yadkin

Creek Confederacy   Georgia
Creek
Hitchiti ("looking upstream")
Kasihta

Manahoac Confederacy   Northern Virginia
Manahoac ("they are very merry")
Hassinunga
Ontponea
Shackaconia

Stegarakes
Tanxnitania ("little")
Teginateo
Whonkentia

Monacan Confederacy   Virginia
Massinicac
Mohemencho
Monacan ("digging stick")
Monahassano
Monisiccapano

Powhatan Confederacy

These tribes were exclusively in Virginia, on land from the coast westward to a little north of Fredericksburg, south to Petersburg and east again to the coast

Accohanoc
Accomac ("across the other side place")
Appamatoc
Arrohatoc
Chesapeake ("country on a great river")
Chickahominy ("coarse corn people")
Chiskiac
Cuttatawoman
Kecoughtan
Mattaponi
Moraughtacund
Mummapacune
Nansamond ("one who goes to fish")
Nantaughtacund
Onawmanient
Pamunkey ("sloping hill")
Paspahegh
Pataunek
Piankatank

Pissasec
Potomac
Powhatan ("falls in a current")
Quioncohanoc
Rappahannock ("alternating stream")
Secacawoni
Tauxenent
Warrasqueoc ("swamp in a depression")
Weanoc
Werowocomoco
Wicocomoco
Youghtanund

Timucuan Confederacy   Northern Florida
Marracon
Mayaca
Potano
Saturiba
Timucua ("lord" or "ruler")
Tocobaga
Yustaga

Miscellaneous Tribes
Acuera   Ocklawahee River, Florida
Agua Dulce ("fresh water")   Florida east coast
Ais   Florida east coast
Amacano   Florida
Amacapiras   Florida southwest coast
Appalachee   North Florida border
Appalachicola ("people on other side") Florida border into Geor-
                                          gia
Bear River   North Carolina
Calusa ("fierce people")   Southern Florida and Keys
Chatot   Georgia
Cherokee ("cave people")   North and South Carolina,
                                          Georgia, Virginia
Chilucan   North Carolina
Chine   Florida
Chowanoc   North Carolina

Combahee	South Carolina
Coree	North Carolina
Croatan	Roanoke Island, North Carolina
Eno ("disliked")	North and South Carolina
Hatteras	Cape Hatteras, Florida
Kanawha	West Virginia
Kayauwee	North and South Carolina
Koasati	Florida
Lumbee	North Carolina
Machapunga	North Carolina
Meherrin	Virginia, North Carolina
Miccosukee	Florida
Moheton	Southwest Virginia˙
Moneton ("big water people")	West Virginia
Moratok	North Carolina
Nottaway ("adders")	Virginia, North Carolina
Ocak	Florida
Oconee	Florida, Georgia
Ofogoula	Georgia
Pamlico	North Carolina
Pensacola ("hair people")	Around Pensacola, Florida
Roanoke	North Carolina
Saluda	South Carolina
Seminole	Florida
Tawasa	Florida
Tequesta	Florida
Tuscarora ("hemp gatherers")	North Carolina
Weapemeoc	North Carolina
Yamasee	Florida, South Carolina, Georgia
Yuchi ("situated yonder")	Florida, South Carolina, Georgia

Major Linguistic Stocks
Iroquoian
Algonquian
Siouan
Muskhogean
Uchean
Timucuan
Arawakan

INDIAN RESERVATIONS OF THE SOUTH ATLANTIC COAST

VIRGINIA
    Pamunkey   King William county
    Mattaponi   King William county

NORTH CAROLINA
    Cherokee   Jackson county
    Lumbee   Robeson county

SOUTH CAROLINA
    Catawba   York county

FLORIDA
    Seminole (three reservations)   Broward, Hendry, and Glades counties

    Miccosukee   Dade county

Non-reservation Communities

VIRGINIA
    Chickahominy   New Kent and Charles City counties

    Rappahannock   Caroline and King and Queen counties

    Potomac   Stafford county
    Accohanoc   Northampton county
    Accomac   Northampton county
    Nansemonds   Norfolk area
    Mixed tribes   Stafford county

GEORGIA
    Cherokee-Creek   Burke county

Indians of the South

Wherever land is fertile there will be people, and throughout the warm climate of the South there were many small tribes and some very large ones. The southern Indians were primarily agriculturists and not too much engaged in warfare. White intrusion disrupted their way of life and the smaller groups passed out of existence or merged with others.

There were no Indians living in Kentucky except in the most southern part. These were the Shawnees, who did not stay there long. It was not by whimsy that Kentucky was named "the dark and bloody ground," for it was an open battlefield for warring tribes who could fight there without damage to their villages.

The expanding colonies at first did not move into an area without permission or direction of the Indian tribes dominating it. In early colonial history, it was not a matter of pushing westward, trampling and stamping over any Indian people in the way. This was to take place later. At first, lands were obtained through purchase and grant, and movement was cautious. It was some time before a trail was forged into the Kentucky wilderness.

The Creek Indians, so prominent in Georgia, were even more so in Alabama. The Creeks revolted against the United

States in 1813 and the Creek War lasted for about a year. General Andrew Jackson and his Cherokee allies completely defeated the Creeks in the famous Battle of Horseshoe Bend. More than 3,000 Creeks were killed. As the price for restoring peace, Jackson demanded the cession of 22 million acres of Creek lands.

The broken Creeks joined in the exodus to Indian Territory with the Cherokees, Chickasaws, Choctaws, and Seminoles. Because these tribes were so highly advanced, or became advanced in white ways and culture, they became known as the Five Civilized Tribes.

Tascalusa was chief of the Alibamu, one of the Creek confederated tribes, when De Soto appeared among them in 1540. He was a very tall man, a veritable giant, strong, well-built, and of handsome features. He bore himself with haughty dignity. When De Soto met Tascalusa, he was seated on a raised platform covered with skins. His son was at his side. The Spaniards, showing off, paraded their horses and put them through a drill, but Tascalusa was unimpressed and watched the proceedings with contempt.

He listened to the Spaniards unwillingly, but when they threatened him, he said that he would send a message to the town of the Mobiles, telling them to welcome the newcomers. Instead, he sent word to call in all fighting men and to be prepared to defend the stockaded town.

The Spaniards were welcomed with singing and dancing. But some noticed that armed Indians were hiding under the rooftops. De Soto was warned and sent for Tascalusa to question him. An attempt to seize the chief precipitated a battle and the Spaniards were driven from the town, followed by the Indians.

In the open country, the Spaniards were better able to defend themselves and they made use of their horses to trample the Indians down. Also, they had swords, lances, and armor, and Indian weapons were no match for these. The Indians were driven back into the town, which was set on fire, and men, women, and children fought on in the flames. The Indians lost 2,500 people while the Spaniards had only 580 wounded. The fate of Tascalusa was never known, but the body of his young son was found, pierced by a lance. This battle has been described by historians as the greatest of the Indian battles ever fought. The Alibamu later removed to Louisiana and eastern Texas.

The Coushattas were strongly allied with the Alibamu and were first mentioned in the chronicles of De Soto. Their principal village was on an island in the Tennessee River and the tribe numbered about 2,000.

De Soto's men robbed them of their corn and seized the chief and twelve others, putting them in chains and threatening to put them to death if they resisted further robbery. The tribe began to migrate southward to escape slave raids from northern tribes, finally joining the Alibamu in Alabama. The two became the center of intensive French effort to win them as military allies and to secure trading privileges. When France ceded her possessions in the area to Spain and England, the protective relationship ended in a shambles.

The American Revolution brought a new and more tragic era, for land-hungry trespassers, encouraged by the states and without the restraints of England's Indian policy, flooded the country. After years of strife and turmoil, Washington invited the Creek tribes to New York to negotiate a peace treaty and the Coushattas gained status as an important tribe.

Red Shoes, their chief, was said to be one of the five most influential chiefs of that time, either in peace or war. The Treaty of New York marked the first formal agreement between the Creek tribes and the United States. It was very disturbing to the Spanish colonial government, which redoubled effort to maintain a hold on Indian loyalty.

When the 31° parallel was established as the line between American and Spanish territorial claims, the Coushattas were up against harsh new political realities. For the first time they were without a secure source of guns and ammunition and without a powerful European ally. It was then that Red Shoes and his followers departed for Louisiana, seeking to find a new home under the protection of Spain. The Coushattas that remained in Alabama saw their land further eaten away and they, too, migrated farther west in search of unspoiled country and Spanish protection. Some of them went as far as Texas.

The Creek War brought to a violent climax the disintegration of the remaining Coushattas as it did of the whole confederacy. With the removal of the Creeks to Indian Territory, the Coushattas accompanied them.

The migration of Red Shoes and his band was a momentous event in the tribal history, for it prepared the way for the establishment of the tribe in Louisiana where the people endured great hardship to preserve their identity. For the next ninety years they would be forced by changing circumstances to move again and again, but Louisiana was to remain their home and their refuge.

Within ten years, the Coushattas in Louisiana had more than tripled in number but now they were caught up in the international struggle for control west of the Mississippi. They were the pawns in American, Spanish, and French politics, and their destiny depended on which side won out.

The Coushattas were drawn by the United States into the War of 1812 and a force of 300 Coushattas and Alibamus combined with American troops at the Battle of San Salado and took part in the capture of San Antonio.

By 1820, the Coushattas were the largest tribe in Louisiana next to the Caddos. Those in East Texas prospered but their fortunes declined with the outbreak of the Texas Revolution.

While they took no part in the fighting, they did slaughter their livestock to feed the starving women and children fleeing from Santa Ana's advancing Mexican army.

Because the Texans feared that the Coushattas would be subverted by the Mexicans, they began to press for their removal from the area, but legislation introduced in the Texas Congress for their removal failed. Nevertheless, they were dispossessed of their Texas lands and many of them returned to Louisiana.

With the annexation of Texas, the Coushattas were now wards of the federal government. With the help of Sam Houston, they tried to secure the land promised them years before "in consideration of their service to their country and their devotion to the early settlers of Texas." They were granted 640 acres, but the descriptive terms were so vague that the land could never be located. Although there were only 80 Coushattas in the state, efforts to move them were renewed and whatever hope existed for rebuilding their community vanished with the Civil War.

Now fairly well settled in Louisiana, the tribe continued its ancient traditions and seemed to be on friendly terms with its neighbors until settlers forced the Indians to move again, for the last time. They were helped to secure vacant land on Bayou Blue, which they purchased, and in 1884 most of the tribe had moved to this location.

In the 1930's the Bureau of Indian Affairs assumed responsibility for the education of the Coushatta children, paying for their tuition in parish schools. In 1940, a federal school was operated for them and medical services were provided. In 1953, the Bureau of Indian Affairs invited the tribe to adopt a resolution agreeing to the termination of federal services, but this was declined. The meager services were discontinued, however.

The Coushattas are in poor condition. Their education and

health status is much below that of the nation at large and their rate of unemployment is higher than 50 per cent. Their housing and sanitation facilities are very poor.

In 1972 they began a renewed effort to win restoration of federal services and fulfillment of federal treaty and other legal obligations. The state of Louisiana accorded them recognition as a tribe and the Indian Health Service agreed to extend them medical services once more. In 1973 the tribe formed a corporation under Louisiana law, modeled on the requirements of the Bureau of Indian Affairs, as a prelimiinary requirement to a request for formal recognition. The tribe has also acquired a tract of land for tribal purposes and plans additional land acquisitions. This is the first land the Coushattas have had title to since the founding of the republic.

The Choctaws and Chickasaws of the Muskhogean family are closely related in language and custom. Their legends tell that they were once a united people who followed two brothers on a long migration from Old Mexico. They crossed the Mississippi River and gave it the name of "father of waters." The Choctaws settled in Mississippi and the Chickasaws went on to Tennessee.

Of the two, the Chickasaws were the more warlike and were noted for their bravery and independence of spirit. They were enemies of the French and their first treaty was with the United States. They began to move west of the Mississippi as early as 1822.

Of all the southern Indians, the Choctaws were the most agricultural. They were courageous fighters, but most of their fighting was defensive in nature. They were allies of the French until the English traders succeeded in establishing themselves in some of their eastern towns. This brought on a civil war in the tribe and a divided relationship. When the French relinquished their territory, the Choctaws began to move west. After ceding most of their lands to the United States, the tribe as a whole removed to Indian Territory in 1832.

Pushmataha was a noted Choctaw who was born in Mississippi. He was distinguished as a brave before he was twenty, when he took five scalps in a single-handed encounter with the Osage. This won him a chieftaincy and he had much influence in promoting friendly relations with the whites.

When Tecumseh visited the Choctaws in 1811 in an attempt to persuade them to join in an uprising against the Americans, it was Pushmataha who "stood in his path" and held his people neutral. He said that "the Choctaws took the hand of Washington and said they would always be friends of his nation." He could not go against his forefathers or be false to their promises.

In the Creek War, Pushmataha was at the head of 500 Choctaw warriors and served in twenty-four campaigns. He was such a rigid disciplinarian that he made efficient soldiers of his men and became known as the "Indian general." On a trip to Washington to negotiate a treaty for his tribe, he became ill with the croup and died in a few hours. He was buried with full military honors in Congressional Cemetery in Washington. A procession of 2,000 persons, both military and civilian and including President Jackson, accompanied the body to the grave. Jackson often said that "Old Push" was the greatest and bravest Indian he had ever known, and Pushmataha was eulogized by John Randolph in the Senate.

Deeply interested in the education of his people, Pushmataha devoted $2,000 of his war service annuity annually for fifteen years toward support of the schools established by the tribe.

The Natchez were one of the most unusual of all tribes. Almost entirely dependent on agriculture for their livelihood, they were also skilled in arts. From the inner bark of the mulberry tree they wove a textile fabric which they used for clothing. They made excellent pottery and constructed mounds of earth on which they built their dwellings and temples. They were a typical example of an ancient Temple Mound culture continuing to survive, and were ruled by a king whom they believed to be a descendant of the sun. He was called the Great Sun. Every deference and honor was shown to the king, whose rule was absolute except when it came to politics. In such matters, he could make no decision of his own but was subject to the opinions of a council of old men.

The home of the king was on a long, flat-topped mound about ten feet high. Nearby was the temple where the eternal fire was kept burning, and where the sacred bones of other Great Suns were buried. No one could enter the Temple but the Great Sun, who was a high priest, and a few chosen ones who were the fire keepers.

The mother or the sister of the Great Sun was the principal woman Sun and would choose the successor to the Great Sun when he died. Relatives were known as Little Suns and from them two war chiefs and two masters of ceremonials were chosen. Below the Great Sun was a class of nobles, and below these was a class of honored men. The commoners were the lowest of all and they were badly treated by the others and humiliated with the name of Stinkards. Strangely enough, all Suns, both great and little, could marry only commoners.

The female Sun had an all-important, behind-the-scenes power. Her husband had to stand in her presence and was never allowed to sit with her. If he somehow displeased her, she could have killed him at the snap of her fingers, and if he was no longer favorable in her eyes, she could have him thrown out of her house.

The Natchez people flattened their heads to a point—by placing a binding around the head in infancy—and wore their hair in bizarre fashion. One side of the head might be shaved, for example, with long, flowing locks on the other side. Bodies were heavily tattooed from the face to the ankles, and the men carried fans.

The Great Sun wore a crown of swan feathers tasseled in scarlet. He was carried about on a litter with a platform which had a bolster made of goose feathers and which was heaped with the finest of buffalo robes and bearskins.

The last of the Natchez war chiefs was Tattooed Serpent, the brother of the Great Sun, who was greatly beloved. When he died, the power and glory of the Natchez began to die also.

When De Soto arrived, he told the Natchez that he was the "brother of the sun." They replied that they would believe him if he dried up the Mississippi River, a test he naturally failed. The Spaniards were therefore not welcome in Mississippi. The French, however, colonized among the Natchez, were readily accepted, and obtained large tracts of land for their plantations.

For a time, all was harmonious. Then a new French commander named Chepart came and was a villian in every sense of the word. He tyrannized everyone, both Indian and French, and was thoroughly hated. When he seized the village of the Great Sun for his own plantation, and demanded high tribute from the people, the Indians could bear no more.

In secret, the Natchez appealed to the Choctaw, some of whom were against the French, and got their promise of help. But the western Choctaws still held to their French loyalties and betrayed the plan. Without the promised help, the Natchez were not strong enough to fight alone, although they tried bravely. When they were eventually defeated, many of the people were burned in a public display, and others, with the Great Sun, were sold into slavery in Santo Domingo. The remaining few then went into exile and lived among the Chickasaws, Creeks, and Cherokees, where they were looked upon as mystics because of their ancient religion and claim of relationship to the sun.

The Alabama-Coushatta Indians live on the only reserved lands for Indians in East Texas, not far from Houston. A few years ago the Tribal Council decided to start a number of tourism projects and their venture has been highly successful.

For many years, this group was isolated on the 1,280-acre reservation arranged for them by General Sam Houston in 1854. Their culture almost gone, the Indians aspired to do something with themselves, and they possessed a good deal of common sense.

First of all, they recreated an Indian village, relearned some of the old dances, and demonstrated Indian baking, beadwork, pottery making, woodcraft, bow and arrow making, and leathercraft. Indians in costume conduct tours through the village and relate tribal history. They also conduct motorized tours into the wooded area known as the "Big Thicket," which follow trails used for generations by Indian people. The forest is exceptional for that region of Texas and contains unusual trees, all identified. A part of the "Big Thicket" is explored by a miniature train, also operated by tribesmen.

In addition, the Indians operate a snack bar, a museum, a reptile farm, and have set up barbecue pits and picnic tables. Future plans call for a restaurant, an amphitheatre where a pageant based on tribal history will be presented, and a grocery and service station. Facilities for campers and trailers already exist.

TRIBES OF THE SOUTH

(Kentucky, Tennessee, Alabama, Louisiana, Mississippi, Arkansas, East Texas)

Caddo Confederacy

Arkansas, Louisiana, eastern Texas

Adai
Anadarko
Doustioni
Eyeish
Hainai
Kadohadacho (Caddo) ("real Caddo")
Nabedache ("salt")
Nacaniche
Nacogdoches
Nakanawan
Nanatsoho
Nasoni
Natchitoches
Ouachita
Quapaw ("downstream people")
Yatasi

Creek Confederacy

Alabama

Abihka
Alibamu (Alabama) ("I open, or clear the thicket")
Coushatta (Koasati)
Hilibi
Huhliwahli ("to apportion war")
Kawita
Kusa
Muskogee
Wakokai

Karankawa Confederacy

Eastern Texas

Ebahamo
Emet
Kouyam

Meracouman
Quara
Quinet

Miscellaneous Tribes

Aculapissa ("those who listen and see")	Mississippi, Louisiana
Ahehouen	East Texas
Appalachicola ("people of the other side")	Alabama
Arhau	East Texas
Avoyelles ("people of the rocks")	Louisiana, Texas
Bayogoula ("bayou people")	Louisiana
Biloxi ("first people")	Mississippi
Cahinnio	Arkansas
Capinans	Mississippi
Chaquantic	Louisiana
Chickamauga	Tennessee
Chickasaw	Tennessee, Alabama, Mississippi
Chitimacha ("they possess cooking pots")	Mississippi
Choctaw ("separation")	Mississippi
Chorruco	East Texas
Coaque	East Texas
Doguenes	East Texas
Grigra	Mississippi
Han	East Texas
Houma ("red")	Louisiana, Alabama
Ibitoupa	Mississippi
Kabaye	East Texas
Kiabaha	East Texas
Kopano	East Texas
Koroa	East Texas
Mariames	East Texas
Mendica	East Texas
Mobile	Alabama
Moctobi	East Texas
Napoche	East Texas
Natchez	Mississippi
Ointemarhen	East Texas
Omenaosse	East Texas
Pascagoula ("bread people")	Mississippi

Shawnee ("southerners")	Kentucky
Taensa	Alabama, Louisiana
Tangipahoa ("herb gatherers")	Louisiana
Taposa	Mississippi, Louisiana
Tawakoni ("river bend among red sand hills")	East Texas
Tiou	Mississippi
Tohome	Alabama
Tunica ("the people")	Mississippi
Waco	East Texas
Washa	Louisiana
Yamasee ("gentle")	Alabama
Yazoo	Mississippi

Major Linguistic Stocks
Muskhogean
Siouan
Natchesan
Tonikan
Chitimachan
Attacapan
Karankawan
Caddoan

INDIAN RESERVATIONS IN THE SOUTH

MISSISSIPPI
    Choctaw   Neshoba county

LOUISIANA
    Coushatta   Calcasieu, Allen, and Jefferson Davis parishes

    Charenton (Chitimacha)   East Baton Rouge parish
    Houma   Terrebonne and Lafourche parishes

    Tunica-Biloxi   Avoyelles parish

EAST TEXAS
    Alabama-Coushatta   Polk county

Non-reservation Communities

LOUSIANA
    Choctaw   Saint Tammany, Rapides, and La Salle parishes

    Attakapa   Calcasieu parish

ALABAMA
    Creek   Escambia county

Indians of the Central States

The Indians of the central states were also woodland Indians, following much the same pattern of life as those of the eastern coast. In this section of the country, however, the round bark wigwams were more numerous and there were no palisaded or fortified towns.

The people hunted and fished, raised their crops and gathered wild plants, especially wild rice, which was a staple food in the lakes area. They made maple sugar in the early spring. They were expert canoeists.

Throughout this region, many mounds are found—the remains of previous Indian civilizations dating back into lost centuries. The Mound Builders eventually disappeared and the tribes, as we came to know them, had no knowledge or memory of them.

The mound building cultures are said to have had their greatest development thousands of years ago. These people formed an elaborate society that appears to have centered in the heart of the Ohio Valley, spreading along the Mississippi and throughout the central region. Evidences of the Mound Builders are found from the Gulf of Mexico to Minnesota and from Ohio to Kansas.

The people built great burial mounds and extensive earthwork systems. Their towns or ceremonial centers were along the riverways and they traded for pipestone, shells, and metals from the Rockies to the Atlantic. They made artifacts of excellent workmanship from wood, mica, and copper.

Some of the mounds were conical or round in shape. Others, called effigy mounds, were in the form of birds, animals, or other creatures. The Serpent Mound in Ohio is the largest and finest serpent effigy in this country. An embankment of earth, nearly one-fourth of a mile long, the greater part of the body extending in seven deep curves, represents a gigantic serpent in the act of uncoiling. An oval mound at one end is the mouth of the serpent or an egg which it is about to swallow.

Seip Mound, also in Ohio, harbored the richest assortment of artifacts so far discovered in any mound. There were a number of burials and with these were copper breastplates and cloth that was apparently part of splendidly woven robes. The colors of red, maroon, orange, yellow, tan, and black are still bright and strong. Ceremonial pipes and thousands and thousands of fresh-water pearls, pierced and strung and ranging in size from seed pearls to those three-fourths of an inch in diameter, were also found in the mound.

Cahokia Mound in central Illinois, is the largest mound of its type north of Mexico and the largest prehistoric earthen construction in the world. The mound was once part of a city covering about six square miles with a population of between 30,000 and 40,000. It was first inhabited in 700 A.D. by Indians who lived in compact villages, hunted and fished, gathered wild plants, and practiced some gardening.

They were replaced by a new people who depended on a well-developed agricultural system with corn, beans, and squash as the main cultivated crops. They also hunted and fished. Because they had a strong, stable, and year-round economy, they were able to develop a complex social and religious structure, which vanished before the early explorers came to America. This culture, known as the Temple Mound Builders, was still followed to a degree by the Natchez of Mississippi when discovered by the Spanish.

The city of Cahokia had a large residential area. Houses were arranged along streets or around plazas. About 1150 A.D. a stockade twelve to fifteen feet high enclosed some 300 acres of the city and two more walls were later built. More than 15,000 logs were used for this structure.

There were probably more than one hundred smaller mounds in the vicinity of Cahokia but the sites of only eighty-six have been located. Forty are preserved in Cahokia State Park. Nearly 50 million cubic feet of earth were moved to build these entirely earthen mounds. The soil was broken up with digging tools made of wood, shell, and stone, and transported to sites in baskets or skin bags.

Cahokia has a flat top, which was a base for ceremonial buildings or for the homes of priests and leading men. The mound base covers fourteen acres, which is slightly larger than that of the great pyramid of Cheops in Egypt. It rises in four terraces to a height of 100 feet and a very large building once stood on the fourth terrace.

The excavation of a nearby mound revealed the burial of a ruler laid on a cape or blanket encrusted with more than 20,000 pearl disk beads. It was surrounded by the bodies of attendants and those of other men and women. Some of these were sacrificial. A copper staff, fifteen finely-made game stones, a basketload of mica, and some 800 arrowheads were also found.

The sites of four circular sun calendars of large, evenly-spaced log posts were uncovered too. These were used to predict changing seasons, perhaps to determine certain ceremonial periods which would be important to an agricultural way of life. They bear silent witness to the abilities in science and engineering of the Cahokia people.

One of the most important sites in Indian history is in this central region. This is Pipestone Quarry in Minnesota. It was here that the area tribes got the beautiful red stone from which they made their pipes used for ceremonials and to bind treaties. Once formalized by the smoking of the pipe, a treaty or agreement could never be broken. The quarry is said to have been the most important single location in Indian geography in recent times. The Dakota Indians especially frequented the spot and traded the pipes they made with Indians as far away as the Southwest, Mississippi, and North Carolina.

Pipestone Quarry figured in treaties made with the Dakota, who claimed ownership. The last treaty was with the Yanktons and their full claim to ownership was settled for $28,508. Only Indians are now allowed to remove any pipestone, and then only if it is to be used for pipes. The quarry is reserved and protected for them for as long as they wish.

In the central states there was much shifting about as tribes warred with one another. Some moved in as migrants pushed westward by stronger tribes in the East or by the enlarging frontier. They changed their places of settlement as they came in conflict with tribes already resident there.

Those living on the western fringe were gradually driven out onto the plains where they developed an entirely new way of life.

The Chippewa, or Ojibwa, as they called themselves, was the largest tribe north of Mexico. They were named for their moccasin style, which made use of a puckered seam. Of the Algonquian family, the Chippewa ranged widely over the country along both shores of Lakes Huron and Superior to as far west as the Turtle Mountains in North Dakota. They moved about from village to village with the seasons, and probably because of their remoteness from the frontier they never became prominent in American history.

The first tribe in the area to secure firearms from the French, they immediately began to drive out the Dakotas. Originally from the East, the Dakotas had been pushed out by larger tribes and had wandered westward. Although they were courageous fighters, they could not stand up against guns and so moved out onto the plains where they established a new way of life, and in time became dominant.

The word Dakota, or Lakota, meaning friends or allies, was their own name and referred to their five large divisions, which in turn were divided into a number of well-known bands. When the French first saw them, they asked the Chippewa who the strange Indians were and were told, "Nadowessioux—they are snakes, or enemies." The French took this to be the tribal name and, shortened to Sioux, it has remained in continued use as such, although much disliked by the Dakota people, who are trying to revive their original name.

The Chippewa were also constantly at war with the Mesquakies (Fox) and drove them out of Wisconsin along with the Sauk (Sac). The two joined to form the Sac and Fox tribe. They had a loose confederacy with the Ottawa and Potawatomi and generally acted with them in unison. Still a large tribe, the Chippewa today are the fourth largest group in the country.

The Hurons, originally a confederation of Iroquoian tribes, migrated to Michigan from Ontario. Unlike the Five Nations, they were friendly to the French, who called them "the good Iroquois."

The Hurons, too, were a very large tribe with some thirty towns. Some of these were palisaded and others were fortified with long pieces of timber standing in triple rows and interlaced with one another to a height of sixteen feet. They were reinforced on the inside with broad coarse strips of bark and large trees, with their branches lopped off, laid lengthwise. There were platforms at intervals reached by crude ladders. Here stones were piled for hurling and water was stored to put out fires.

The Hurons planted very large fields of several kinds of corn and many varieties of beans. They funneled through to French trading posts canoe-flotilla loads of furs taken in trade from the vast country to the north and west of them. When they invited the Jesuit priests to come among them, the anger of the Iroquois exploded. They had long hated the French because of a defeat suffered at the hands of Champlain and they saw the missionaries as a threat to Indian customs. They attacked the Hurons in a surprise move and destroyed several villages, taking many captives.

Although they outnumbered the Iroquois, the Hurons panicked and scattered to the four winds. They finally came to rest around Detroit where they changed their name to Wyandot. They grew in numbers and became very influential in the Ohio Valley. In the War of 1812, they sided with the English against the Americans, for by then the French no longer had any power in the East.

With the peace treaty of 1815, the ownership by the Wyandots of a large tract of land in Ohio and Michigan was acknowledged, and four years later this land was sold except for a small area near Upper Sandusky in Ohio and another near Detroit. Later, the Wyandots moved to Kansas and then to Indian Territory. A few still reside in Canada.

The Winnebagos were first discovered by the French explorer Nicolet. Thinking he had reached China, Nicolet came among them wearing Mandarin robes and firing pistols, which no doubt made an impression. Like other tribes of the lakes area, the Winnebagos came under French influence and had a friendly relationship with them.

The Winnebagos were great travelers and they tell of having visited the Atlantic coast where they saw a giant canoe with huge sails come to shore. Living near Green Bay, these Indians possessed valuable lead mines and they mined and processed lead, decorating their pipes, for one thing, with lead inlay.

With the coming of the settlers, envious eyes were cast upon these mines and a way was found to deprive the Indians of them and to drive them out of Wisconsin. At bayonet point, the Indians were pushed into Minnesota where they established themselves and were becoming prosperous. With the Sioux Uprising that took place in 1862, there was a hue and cry for the removal of all Indians, and the Winnebagos, though they were peaceful throughout, were again driven from their homes. They fled to Nebraska and were taken in by the Omahas, with whom they now share a reservation.

Some of the people made their way back to Wisconsin and evaded all attempts to dislodge them. There are Winnebagos still living who remember hiding in the woods from the soldiers, and covering their footsteps by dragging bundles of leafy branches behind them. The Wisconsin Winnebagos have no reservation but are scattered through several counties in the state.

No history of the central states can be complete without mention of a trio of Indians who were very great men and who deservedly rank as patriots and heroes. Pontiac, who loved the French and hated the English, was an Ottawa. Tecumseh, the "shooting star" of the Shawnee, was determined to preserve the lands of the Ohio Valley for all Indians. Black Hawk, of the Sauk and Fox, sought to remain on the land of his birth and in the village he loved so dearly.

The Ottawa Indians were noted traders. They were also great warriors, fishermen, and hunters, and strongly tied to the French who lived among them. Pontiac's village was close to Fort Detroit. Little is known of his childhood except that he grew up thinking of the French as his brothers. He had many friends at the fort who welcomed him cordially and there was much visiting between Detroit and the Indian village. The French joined in Indian games and feasts and the Indians were invited to balls and parties at the fort. Each could speak the other's language.

Pontiac's father was a chief who did not take to French ways as the other Indians did. He brought his son up as an Indian and all his life he remained one. His own father had impressed upon him that Indians would destroy their native strengths and themselves if they gave up their self-reliance and became too dependent on the possessions of the white man. But the Ottawas wanted the goods and guns of the whites and they refused to listen to any words of warning. They sold themselves to the French, becoming more French than Indian.

When Pontiac was quite young, he defended Fort Detroit from attack by the Chippewas, who had been played upon by the English seeking to take over the Michigan territory and who had become discontent with the French association. He also led the French and Indians in the battle in which the British general, Braddock, was defeated and killed in an attempt to capture Fort Dusquesne. There was never any doubt that he was "French Pontiac" and he said that he would "stand in the path" of the English so that they would never come into what was then the Northwest Territory.

However, the French lost their war in Europe with the English and, as part of the surrender, gave up all their lands in Canada and to the Mississippi. Pontiac was present when the French flag came down at Fort Detroit, his face blackened in mourning. He said farewell to the commandant, but pledged that he would be at war with the English in his heart forever. He promised that he would find a way to bring the French back and the French promised that they would help him.

Under the English, the old happy times and warm close relationships were soon gone. The English were harsh and arrogant, and the Indians suffered because they could no longer rely on themselves and could obtain trade goods only with difficulty.

Pontiac began to make his plans to unite the lake tribes to attack the English and destroy their settlements. He promised the help of the French and he was successful in winning the support of a goodly number of tribes. His military strategy was brilliant. Like King Philip, he arranged that on a given day at a certain time, the tribes would separately and suddenly attack all of the English forts. Most of the forts fell to the Indians except Detroit and Fort Pitt and these were never taken.

As the fighting went on, the Indians became discouraged. They wanted to return to their homes for the seasonal hunting. When the promised help did not come from the French, they abandoned Pontiac and his cause and made their own peace with the English. The French advised Pontiac that he, too, must make peace, for they had entered into a treaty with England and could not break it, and finally Pontiac was forced to give up. He withdrew from Detroit and went to live in Ohio. Then, lonesome for his French friends, he journeyed to St. Louis to visit those living there. This aroused the mistrust of the English, who had never quite trusted Pontiac anyway. On his way home, while staying in a Cahokia village, he was killed by a Kaskaskia Indian in the pay of the English.

Pontiac's death aroused the lake tribes to vengeance and they fell upon the Illini tribes in a war of extermination. At last only a pitiful handful remained who took refuge with the French settlers.

*   *   *

Tecumseh was born near Springfield, Ohio. When he was a child, his village was destroyed by Kentuckians, and later his father was killed in a battle with the settlers. Tecumseh was then raised by an older brother who was also killed in battle on the Tennessee frontier. Still another brother was killed, with Tecumseh fighting at his side, in the famous Battle of Fallen Timbers with "Mad Anthony" Wayne.

It is no wonder that Tecumseh's hatred for all whites was intense. He had become a distinguished warrior, well known for his bravery and also for his humanitarianism. He influenced his tribe to give up their custom of torturing prisoners, and he would never harm, or permit the harming of, a woman or child, even those of the race he hated.

Tecumseh opposed any advance on the part of the settlers, insisting that the Ohio River must be the boundary line between the two races, and defying the government in attempts to buy lands from single tribes. He said that the Ohio Valley belonged to all the tribes living there.

When the government refused to acknowledge this, Tecumseh undertook—as Pontiac had done—to form a confederation of the tribes that would fight to keep the Ohio River country for their own. He traveled far and wide, to the west and to the south, and won many to his cause. It was all to come to nothing when his brother, known as The Prophet, precipitated a disastrous battle with General William Henry Harrison at Tippecanoe. The Shawnees were badly defeated, and this caused other Indians to lose faith in Tecumseh.

In 1812, Tecumseh at once declared his support of the English and was commisisoned a brigadier general in the British army. He had under him some 2,000 warriors and his name was so feared that battles were won simply because it was known that he was taking part in them. Then, the American naval officer, Perry, won a great victory on Lake Erie, and the English decided to retreat. Tecumseh protested this and, finally, with the army at the Thames River in Ontario, he refused to retreat farther and forced the English to make a stand. In this battle, the Americans were victorious, and Tecumseh fell at the front of his warriors. He was removed that night and buried in a secret place. His grave was discovered in recent years on Walpole Island.

Just before the battle, Tecumseh changed from his English uniform into his Indian deerskins. He seemed to have a feeling that he was to die. Historians say that he was the most extraordinary Indian in our history.

Black Hawk was a Sauk who was born in the village of Saukenuk in Illinois near the present site of Rock Island. This was one of the largest of Indian villages in the country, and here the Indians had about 800 acres of cultivated fields. The land around the village was covered with blue grass; there were several fine springs, and an abundance of fish in the river. About 100 lodges housed several families each, and the people were never in want. In the early 1820's about 4,000 Sauk Indians lived there.

Black Hawk, too, was a warrior who won fame at an early age. When he was fifteen, he was already a brave and at seventeen he led a party of young men in an attack on an Osage camp. At nineteen, he led 200 Sauk and Fox in an engagement with the Osage.

When his father, who was a medicine man, was killed in a raid on the Cherokees, Black Hawk refrained from going to war for five years. He spent his time trying to secure supernatural powers. When he again went on the warpath, he led a raid against the Cherokees in revenge for the death of his father.

By the terms of a treaty made in 1804, the Sauk and Fox agreed to surrender all of their lands east of the Mississippi but they were permitted to remain there until the country was thrown open for settlement. After the War of 1812, in which Black Hawk fought for the English, the settlers began to pour into Illinois, and the Sauk, under Chief Keokuk, moved into Iowa. Black Hawk refused to go. He said that he was deceived as to the terms of the treaty when he signed it. He planned to fight and tried to enlist the help of the Winnebago and Potawatomi.

There was so much friction that the governor of Illinois finally called out the militia. Black Hawk was summoned to a meeting at Fort Armstrong, but a violent scene took place and nothing was accomplished. As matters worsened, the militia marched on Saukenuk, but all of the people had left. The lodges were burned and it was demanded that the Indians appear for a peace talk. Black Hawk came with twenty-seven others, and finally signed a treaty agreeing to leave.

The following winter Black Hawk, too, laid plans to unite the neighboring tribes and he sent his messengers in all directions, hoping to bring this about. This was in open defiance to Keokuk, whom he tried to undermine as chief or commit to war. At the head of 2,000 followers, only 500 of whom were warriors, Black Hawk once more crossed the Mississippi to his old haunts. But the settlers had been warned by Shabona, a Potawatomi, and once more the militia was called out and pursued Black Hawk up the Rock River. One of those who took part in the struggle with Black Hawk was Abraham Lincoln, who was then a lanky young backwoodsman living in Illinois. These were the first Indians that Lincoln ever saw.

Black Hawk scored a victory over the militia and routed them. He then let loose his followers against the settlements, burning and destroying a number of them. While he was trying to cross the Wisconsin River, he was overtaken by a group of volunteers and badly defeated. He retreated to the Mississippi River near the mouth of the Bad Axe and in attempting to cross was intercepted by the steamboat *Warrior*. His camp was shelled and, in the desperate battle, Black Hawk escaped, only to be captured through the assistance of Winnebago Indians. He was taken to Fortress Monroe in Virginia and held there as a prisoner. Later, he was released and taken on a tour of eastern cities where he was mobbed by crowds all eager to see him.

The tour over, Black Hawk returned to Iowa where he settled down and lived until his death. He was buried in a military uniform presented to him by General Andrew Jackson, with a sword and medals, also from Jackson, and a cane from Henry Clay. Later, his body was stolen and the bones were found in Quincy, Illinois. When the governor of Iowa strongly protested this desecration, the bones were returned and Black Hawk's sons allowed them to remain in the governor's office. They were eventually destroyed in a fire. Black Hawk was the author of a book which related his life story and is still looked upon as a classic.

Little Turtle is still another brilliant chief who should come to attention. A Miami, Little Turtle was remarkable for his military career and for his smashing victories over General Josiah Harmer and General Arthur St. Clair of the American forces in 1790 and 1791.

Little Turtle, a warrior without equal, was born in 1752. He was the leading chief of his tribe and also of the Piankeshaws and Weas. His defeat of St. Clair ranks as one of the most serious defeats ever suffered by the American army. Some 900 American soldiers lost their lives in the battle with St. Clair in a frightful episode. St. Clair was taken completely by surprise and there were survivors only because Little Turtle ordered his men to stop the slaughter.

When Little Turtle reached the age of forty-three, he decided that war was not the way to settle difficulties. He saw that the balance of power was moving against the Indians and that time was on the side of the Americans, for the Indian people were gradually weakening. Like Pontiac, he said that this was due to dependence on white materials, but it was too late for Indians to turn back to their own way of living.

When General Anthony Wayne advanced against the Indians in 1793–94, Little Turtle refused to assist Tecumseh, who asked for his support. He had decided that Wayne was a great soldier and that the Indians could not stand against him. He believed that Indian victories had come to an end, and he urged his tribesmen not to fight. He was then looked upon as a coward and a traitor, and was stripped of all authority as a chief. When his courage was attacked, Little Turtle decided to prove otherwise. He went into battle with the Miamis against Wayne and fought valliantly. But, as he had predicted, the Indians were overcome.

Little Turtle was now an open and firm ally of the Americans. When he signed the treaty of Greenville, he said that he was the last to sign the treaty and would be the last to break it. In return for his loyalty, the government granted Little Turtle a large tract of land near the present site of Fort Wayne. He was given a deed to the land and a large brick house was built for him. He was presented with valuable gifts and grants of money and became the wealthiest man in his community.

George Washington had great respect for him and he was a guest in Washington's home for several weeks. At Washington's request, Little Turtle was vaccinated for smallpox. He learned all about the procedure, for many Indians died of this disease, and when he returned to Indiana he vaccinated a number of his friends.

Just before his death, Little Turtle prevented the Miami from joining forces with the British in the War of 1812. In the spring of that year he died of gout and was given a military funeral by the Americans. A sword given to him by Washington and a pair of pistols from General Kosciusko were buried with him.

TRIBES OF THE CENTRAL STATES

(Ohio, Indiana, Michigan, Wisconsin, Illinois, Minnesota, Iowa, Missouri)

Illiniwek Confederacy — Illinois, Iowa, Missouri
Cahokia
Kaskaskia ("he scrapes it off by means of a tool")
Michagamea ("great water")
Moingwena
Peoria ("he comes carrying a pack on his back")
Tamaroa ("cut tail")

Miscellaneous Tribes

Arapaho	Minnesota
Assiniboine ("he cooks by roasting")	Minnesota
Black Snake	Missouri
°Cherokee ("cave people")	Missouri
Cheyenne ("speak with an alien tongue")	Minnesota
Chippewa (Ojibwa) ("puckered")	Michigan, Minnesota, Wisconsin, North Dakota
°Creek	Missouri
Dakota ("allies")	Minnesota, Wisconsin, Iowa
Santee ("knife")	
Sisseton	
Teton ("prairie men")	
Yankton	
Yanktonnai	
°Delaware	Ohio, Missouri, Wisconsin
°Erie ("panther people")	Michigan, Ohio
Gawkie	Missouri
°Iowa ("sleepy ones")	Minnesota, Iowa, Illinois
Kansa (Kaw)	Missouri
Kickapoo ("stands about")	Wisconsin, Illinois, Missouri

° These are migrant tribes who came into the area and are not native to it.

Mascoutens ("little prairie people")	Wisconsin, Illinois, Indiana
Menominee ("wild rice people")	Wisconsin, Michigan
Mesquakie (Fox) ("red earth people")	Wisconsin, Illinois, Iowa, Missouri
Miami ("people who live on a peninsula")	Indiana, Ohio, Michigan, Wisconsin, Missouri
Missouri ("people having dugouts")	Missouri, Iowa
*Munsee	Missouri, Wisconsin
Neutrals	Michigan
Noquet ("bear foot")	Michigan
Omaha ("going against wind and current")	Iowa, Minnesota
Osage	Missouri
Oto ("lechers")	Minnesota
Ottawa ("traders")	Michigan, Ohio
Pawnee ("horn")	Missouri
Piankeshaw ("those who separate")	Illinois, Missouri, Indiana
Ponca	Iowa, Minnesota
Potawatomi ("people of place of fire")	Michigan, Indiana, Illinois, Wisconsin
Sauk (Sac) ("they who come forth")	Wisconsin, Illinois, Iowa, Missouri
*Shawnee ("southerners")	Ohio, Missouri
*Stockbridge (Mahican)	Wisconsin
Wea ("place of round or carved channel")	Wisconsin, Illinois, Indiana
Winnebago ("filthy water")	Wisconsin, Minnesota
Wyandot (Huron) ("islanders")	Ohio, Indiana, Wisconsin, Missouri, Kansas

Major Linguistic Stocks
Algonquian
Siouan
Iroquoian

INDIAN RESERVATIONS IN THE CENTRAL STATES

MICHIGAN

Bay Mills (Chippewa)	Chippewa county
L'Anse (Chippewa)	Baraga county
Isabella (Chippewa)	Isabella county
Ontonagon (Chippewa)	Ontonagon county

WISCONSIN

Lac du Flambeau (Chippewa)	Vilas and Iron counties
La Pointe (Chippewa)	Apostle Islands
Bad River (Chippewa)	Ashland county
Red Cliff (Chippewa)	Bayfield county
Menominee (Menominee)	Menominee county
Oneida	Brown county
Stockbridge (Stockbridge, Munsee)	Shawano county
Mole Lake (Chippewa)	Forest county
Potawatomi	Forest county
Lac Courte Oreilles (Chippewa)	Sawyer county

MINNESOTA

Fond du Lac (Chippewa)	Saint Louis county
Mille Lacs (Chippewa)	Mille Lacs and Aitken counties
Red Lake (Chippewa)	Beltrami county
Greater Leech Lake (Chippewa)	Cass county
Nett Lake (Chippewa)	Koochiching county
White Earth (Chippewa)	Mahnomen county
Prairie Island (Sioux)	Goodhue county
Lower Sioux	Redwood county
Upper Sioux	Yellow Medicine county
Grand Portage (Chippewa)	Cook county

IOWA

Tama (Sac and Fox)	Tama county

Non-reservation Communities

MICHIGAN

Ottawa	Emmet, Cass, Charlevoix counties

Chippewa

Grand Traverse county, Beaver Island

WISCONSIN
Winnebago

Jackson, La Crosse, Sauk counties

Chippewa

Saint Croix county

INDIANA
Miami

Miami, Wabash, Marion counties

Indians of the Plains
and Mountains

Most of the Plains tribes seem to have come originally from the East, reaching the Plains country only a few hundred years ago. They were pushed westward by stronger tribes as the eastern area became uncomfortably crowded. They continued to live as woodland people until gradually they were pushed out into the open prairie country. For most, their whole way of life had to change. These were the tribes who became true nomads, dependent on the buffalo herds for food and clothing and articles of daily life. They wandered far and wide as the huge beasts wandered, continuously on the move and living in rude shelters.

In earliest times, they went everywhere on foot. Dogs carried the few possessions on drags, and they could not go very far in a day. It was a struggle to survive. Then the Spaniards crossed the southern part of the country and some of their horses escaped and ran away. Wandering horse met wandering Indian and a wonderful new way began.

With the horse, the people could travel many miles and very quickly. Every Indian—man, woman, and child—became expert riders. The horses could pull the drags, called *travois*, and so these became larger and the people could have more possessions. Houses could be larger and clothing better. When the Indians obtained guns, the buffalo could be hunted much more easily and the people enjoyed a prosperity of horses, buffalo skins and robes, and plentiful food.

In this area, no weaving or woodwork was done. Everything, from the house to the smallest item, was made of skin, usually that of the buffalo, or some other part of the great animal. Even boats were made of skin—they were like round tubs.

There were relatively few rivers in the Plains country and they were not important to the horseback Indians as they were to those of the woodlands. The rivers were crossed only when necessary, so that boats were not well developed.

There was no time or inclination to practice agriculture, nor was the land well suited for it. There was no clay for pottery, no material for basketry. Storage cases were made of rawhide, and skins could be painted, so there was much painting in primary colors in flat designs of oblong, square, or triangular shapes. The open country, the freedom of the wind, the horse and the buffalo—these were the world to the tribes of the Plains.

A number of things were distinctive of Plains Indian culture. First was the house—a skin covering stretched over a framework of poles to form a conical dwelling. This was called the *tipi*.

The nomadic life-style required a house that could be swiftly put up and taken down and easily taken along. Strong, slender pines were used for the framework and could only be obtained by a trip to the mountains. The poles were used in the framework of the travois, also. The house was both a shelter and a wagon without wheels.

When camped, the tipis were set up in a large circle, each clan having its set place. When the camp moved, coals of fire

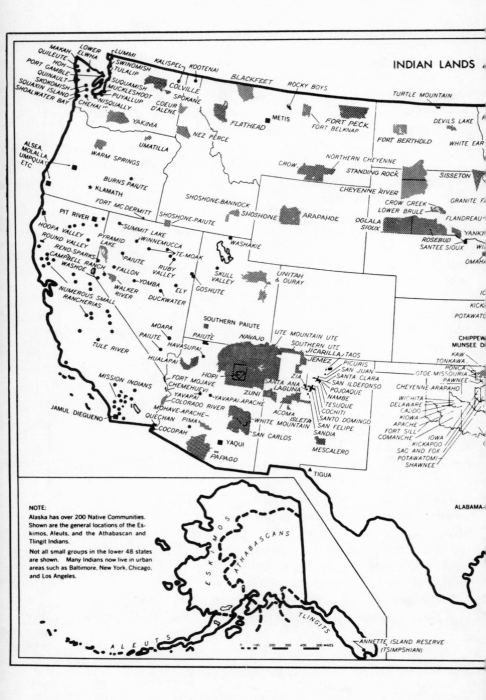

INDIAN LANDS

MAKAN
QUILEUTE
HOH
PORT GAMBLE
QUINAULT
SKOKOMISH
SQUAXIN ISLAND
SHOALWATER BAY
LOWER ELWHA
LUMMI
SWINOMISH
TULALIP
SUQUAMISH
MUCKLESHOOT
PUYALLUP
NISQUALLY
CHEHALIS
KALISPEL
KOOTENAI
COLVILLE
SPOKANE
COEUR D'ALENE
BLACKFEET
ROCKY BOYS
TURTLE MOUNTAIN
YAKIMA
NEZ PERCE
FLATHEAD
METIS
FORT PECK
FORT BELKNAP
FORT BERTHOLD
DEVILS LAKE
WHITE EAR
ALSEA, MOLALLA, UMPQUA, ETC
WARM SPRINGS
UMATILLA
BURNS PAIUTE
KLAMATH
FORT MC DERMITT
SHOSHONE-BANNOCK
NORTHERN CHEYENNE
CROW
STANDING ROCK
CHEYENNE RIVER
CROW CREEK
LOWER BRULE
SISSETON
GRANITE FA
FLANDREAU
PIT RIVER
HOOPA VALLEY
ROUND VALLEY
RENO-SPARKS
CAMPBELL RANCH
WASHOE
SUMMIT LAKE
PYRAMID LAKE
WINNEMUCCA
TE-MOAK
PAIUTE
FALLON
RUBY VALLEY
YOMBA
WALKER RIVER
ELY
DUCKWATER
SHOSHONE-PAIUTE
SHOSHONE
ARAPAHOE
WASHAKIE
SKULL VALLEY
GOSHUTE
UNITAH & OURAY
OGLALA SIOUX
ROSEBUD
SANTEE SIOUX
YANKT
WI
OMAHA
NUMEROUS SMALL RANCHERIAS
TULE RIVER
MOAPA
PAIUTE
PAIUTE
HAVASUPAI
HUALAPAI
SOUTHERN PAIUTE
NAVAJO
UTE MOUNTAIN UTE
SOUTHERN UTE
JICARILLA
TAOS
IC
KICK
POTAWAT
CHIPPEW
MUNSEE D
MISSION INDIANS
JAMUL DIEGUENO
FORT MOJAVE
CHEMEHUEVI
YAVAPAI
MOHAVE-APACHE-COLORADO RIVER
YAVAPAI-APACHE
QUECHAN
COCOPAH
PIMA
HOPI
ZUNI
SANTA ANA
LAGUNA
ACOMA
ISLETA
WHITE MOUNTAIN
SAN CARLOS
YAQUI
PAPAGO
JEMEZ
ZIA
PICURIS
SAN JUAN
SANTA CLARA
SAN ILDEFONSO
POJOAQUE
NAMBE
TESUQUE
COCHITI
SANTO DOMINGO
SAN FELIPE
SANDIA
MESCALERO
TIGUA
KAW
TONKAWA
PONCA
OTOE-MISSOURIA
PAWNEE
CHEYENNE-ARAPAHO
WICHITA
DELAWARE
CADDO
KIOWA
APACHE
FORT SILL
COMANCHE
IOWA
KICKAPOO
SAC AND FOX
POTAWATOMI
SHAWNEE
ALABAMA-

NOTE:
Alaska has over 200 Native Communities. Shown are the general locations of the Eskimos, Aleuts, and the Athabascan and Tlingit Indians.

Not all small groups in the lower 48 states are shown. Many Indians now live in urban areas such as Baltimore, New York, Chicago, and Los Angeles.

ESKIMOS
ATHABASCANS
ALEUTS
TLINGITS
0   100   200   300   400   500 MILES
ANNETTE ISLAND RESERVE (TSIMPSHIAN)

MUNITIES

MALECITE
MICMAC
PASSAMAQUODDY

PENOBSCOT

TT LAKE   GRAND PORTAGE
CH LAKE
         KEEWENAW BAY
CLIFF BAD RIVER   OTTAWA AND CHIPPEWA   BAY MILLS
      LAC COURTE   LAC DU
       OREILLES   FLAMBEAU   MOHAWK
   SOKAOGON
                  HANNAHVILLE   ONEIDA   NIPMUC
  PRAIRIE ISLAND POTAWATOMI   TONOWANDA ONONDAGA   WAMPANOAG
IOUX   WINNEBAGO   ONEIDA   TUSCARORA   NARRAGANSET
       STOCKBRIDGE BROTHERTON ISABELLA   CAYUGA   SENECA   SCATICOOK   MOHEGAN
        MUNSEE   POGAGON   PAUGUSETT   MONTAUK
ND FOX   POTAWATOMI   POTAWATOMI   PEQUOT   SHINNECOCK
                                                                                        POOSEPATUCK

FOX   MIAMI   MOOR
                                                                         NANTICOKE
OT   RAPPAHANOCK
   SHAWNEE   UPPER MATTAPONI
   MIAMI   MATTAPONI
   PEORIA   PAMUNKEY
   QUAPAW   AMHERST   CHICKAHOMINY
   SENECA-CAYUGA   HALIWA
   WYANDOTTE
                                                CUBAN
                               CHEROKEE   COHARIE
                                                              LUMBEE
                               CATAWBA   WACCAMAW

                               SUMMERVILLE

               CHOCTAW

HOCTAW
              CHOCTAW   CREEK
AW   TUNICA
  COUSHATTA
HITIMACHA
     HOUMA
                                              SEMINOLE
                                                      SEMINOLE
                                                     SEMINOLE
                                                     MICCOSUKEE
               LEGEND   MICCOSUKEE

• FEDERAL INDIAN RESERVATIONS
▲ State Indian Reservations
■ Other Indian Groups
★ Terminated (Only Menominee and Klamath shown)

0   100   200   300   400   500 MILES
ALBERS EQUAL AREA PROJECTION

BUREAU OF INDIAN AFFAIRS—1971

were carried in a buffalo horn and kept aglow so that new fires could be lighted at the next camping place without delay.

Second—the great use of eagle feathers and the head-dresses of these feathers which were the warriors' "crowning glory." They signified that the wearer had won many war honors. Such headdresses could not have been worn in wooded country.

Third—the sign, or hand gesture, language, developed so that tribes not understanding each other could meet and talk. There was also a touch language used by scouts or men on the warpath when close to the enemy.

When beads were obtained from the early traders, the Plains Indians created their own style, differing from others in designs and method. Beadwork was a craft that could be easily taken along on travels and it became a high art. Everything that could be beaded was beaded, the beads replacing the flattened porcupine quills that had formerly been used for decoration.

Some of the tribes that lived on the fringes of the Plains country had features combining both Plains and Woodland cultures—more of one or the other or equally of both. They continued to practice agriculture and lived in permanent villages, hunting the buffalo in certain seasons. They dressed in the Plains style and became warlike. In some areas they lived in earth lodges that were built partially underground, with rounded mounds of earth covering them. On the southern Plains, some of the tribes built large round houses of grass.

The typical Plains Indian has come to be romanticized as the typical Indian of America, but actually there was no typical Indian. Even within cultures there was great variety. The Plains tribes represent a very small segment of the long list of tribes that once inhabited this country.

They were a picturesque people, however, and they had

no peers as fighters. Each of them had a tragic story, as contact with the whites brought violent conflict. Those who were accustomed to roving had perhaps a greater adjustment to make than most tribes, as this freedom was denied them and they were forced to live within the smaller boundaries of a reservation.

The tribes of this area have almost, every one, a similar tragic story, differing only in locale and in some detail but otherwise pretty much the same. Crushed and broken by the contact with whites, these people—born to be free and to whom freedom was the only way of life—were almost beaten into the ground by the confinement of the restricted lands where they were finally forced to live and by having to change over to a new living pattern to which they were emotionally unsuited.

The bitter edge of memory has not entirely worn smooth—perhaps because what happened is not yet so far back in history that images are blurred or dimmed. The shock was etched indelibly on the minds of all, both Indian and white, who witnessed or experienced it. Even hardened military officers were moved to expressions of sorrow.

The establishment of reservations was not done for the purpose of inflicting cruelty. For one thing, it was a protection for both settlers and Indians, who were at each others' throats—both threatened with extinction as one group fought to further goals and the other to defend what was theirs.

By reserving Indian lands, a sanctuary was provided and some property retained. It was obvious that the whites would not be thwarted and, as more and more crowded in, the game on which the Indian depended would leave or die off and the people would no longer be able to sustain themselves in their own way. Also, it was reasoned that Indians were a dying race, succumbing to the diseases of the whites and adjusting to the new order with great difficulty. They would soon vanish with the buffalo, it was believed, so let them have this little for the time that was left.

But Indians did not die off or vanish. They suffered, endured, survived, and grew in numbers to find that the lands determined as theirs were not adequate for their support. This made for even greater hardship, a hardship that still exists in some parts of the Plains country.

In attempting to atone for what was done to a once strong and virile people, again the methods used were not meant to be unkind, but were often strict and harsh, or were serious mistakes made by misguided people.

Of all the tribes of the Plains country, the Sioux are the best known, partly because of the Battle of the Little Big Horn (1876) where General George A. Custer and all of his men were wiped out by Sioux warriors. It was a tremendous Indian victory, but the last they were to have.

The Sioux was a mighty tribe made up of seven divisions and a number of strong bands, each one a name to be reckoned with. They roamed from the Dakotas through Nebraska, Montana, and Wyoming, dominating the entire scene.

Red Cloud is said to have been their most famous and most powerful chief. An Oglala, Red Cloud was born in Nebraska in 1822. A brilliant young warrior, he counted eighty coups or war honors, and became chief through his own force of character and ability.

When the government sought to build a road from Fort Laramie to the gold regions of Montana, Red Cloud gathered together the fighting men and refused to negotiate a treaty or even to attend a council concerning one. He surrounded the troops and the labor force that had begun work on the road with 2,000 warriors and kept up such continual interferences that not even a load of hay could be brought into the fort. Hunting for food was impossible.

Several severe fights took place, with Red Cloud always

coming out the victor. He was finally persuaded to come to a conference, where he demanded the abandonment of the three army posts and of all effort to complete the Montana road. The Treaty of Fort Laramie was finally drawn up in accord with his demands, but Red Cloud would not sign it until the garrisons of the three posts were actually withdrawn and the army gave in. It was no wonder that Red Cloud was so admired by his people.

Red Cloud kept his promise to live in peace but he resisted any introduction of the marks of white civilization. He went to Washington a number of times as a spokesman for his people and visited other cities where care was taken to show him huge crowds. He was surrounded by mobs who hailed him as a great hero, and he was duly impressed by the sheer numbers.

This no doubt influenced him to agree to the cession of the Black Hills, the sacred lands of the Sioux. He felt that it would be impossible for the Indians to hold them and that they would be destroyed in trying to do so. The Indians could not understand what had happened to their courageous leader and felt that he had betrayed them.

Red Cloud's words were proved to be right when gold was discovered in the hills. It became impossible for the military to control the situation or keep the prospectors and settlers out, and the Indians were in a defenseless position.

Red Cloud settled on the reservation which is called Pine Ridge today. This was the scene in 1890 of the baseless and horrible slaughter at Wounded Knee of Big Foot and his band by white soldiers one snowy day shortly before Christmas. Even women, children, and infants were relentlessly killed, and when it was over, the silent bodies lying frozen in the snow were scooped into a single ditch grave. It was here in February, 1972, that a group of modern Indians staged an uprising which, in part, was a protest over unkept provisions to later amendments to the Fort Laramie treaty.

A younger warrior who lived at the time of Red Cloud was Sitting Bull of the Hunkpapa. When he was ten, he killed his first buffalo, and when he was fourteen he went with a war party against the Crows and counted his first war honor. As was the custom, his father held a great feast and feted him as a warrior, giving away many presents and fine horses to pay him honor.

Sitting Bull was active in the Plains wars of the 1870's as Red Cloud was not. He became widely known and was on the warpath almost constantly against the frontier posts and against other tribes. When he refused to live on a reservation, General Custer was sent to round up Sitting Bull and his band. This resulted, in 1876, in the wiping out of Custer and his troops not far from the Crow Reservation in Montana.

Sitting Bull escaped with his people to Canada, but after five years returned and went to live on the Standing Rock Reservation in North Dakota. For a time he traveled with Buffalo Bill's Wild West Show where he was the center of attraction. Shortly after his return to the reservation, the Ghost Dance movement was begun by Wovoka, a Paiute. This promised the Indians who would believe and accept the new religion that the good old days would return, the buffalo would come back, those who had died would live again, and the whites would be gone forever.

These promises were sweet to the disheartened, embittered people, and many of them joined in the Ghost Dance. It was believed that Sitting Bull encouraged it, although he insisted that he did not. However, soldiers were sent to arrest him and in the confusion which took place, he and his son, with other Indians, were killed. The horse which Sitting Bull had ridden in the Wild West Show, hearing the shots, remembered his old act and solemnly went through all his tricks just as if his master were riding him. But his master lay dead, his blood staining the ground, and the wails of his family sounding their anguish instead of the applause the horse was accustomed to hear.

A few days later, the massacre of the Big Foot band occurred as the Indians, terrified by the killing of Sitting Bull, attempted to take refuge in the Dakota Badlands.

There were many among the Sioux who shared in their days of glory. They are too many to mention all, but the name of Crazy Horse must not be overlooked. Crazy Horse was a dashing young brave, leading in the charges against Fort Laramie when Red Cloud was in command. He was also one who played an outstanding role in the defeat of Custer, acting with Sitting Bull as one of the key figures of Indian resistance.

Pursued by General Nelson Miles, Crazy Horse was forced to surrender because his people were starving. When it was thought that he was preparing to stir up another war, he was placed under arrest. Taken by surprise, he tried to pull away from his captors and was killed. A handsome monument to this daring warrior is being carved out of a mountainside near Custer, South Dakota. It shows him mounted on horseback, pointing out over the countryside, remindful of his saying: "My lands are where my dead lie buried."

In modern times, the Sioux people have shown the same ability for leadership as their early great men. There are a goodly number in the various professions; a large number have college educations and there are some with Ph.D's.

The first of the Sioux to carve a name for himself in the white man's world was Dr. Charles A. Eastman. He was brought up in the old buffalo hunting days and was sixteen before he had any contact with whites. Then he attended a mission school and Beloit College, going on to Dartmouth and Boston University where he obtained his medical degree. He was physician for the Sioux at the time of the Wounded Knee massacre.

Retiring from medicine after some years in private practice, Dr. Eastman became an author and lecturer of note. He was a traveling secretary among Indians for the YMCA, acted as an attorney for the Sioux, representing them in Washington, and he revised the land allotment rolls and selected permanent family names for the Sioux people. For example, a man who had the Indian name of Bobbed-tail Coyote was given the name of Robert Taylor Wolf. In 1933, Dr. Eastman was presented the first Indian Achievement Award by the Indian Council Fire at the Chicago Century of Progress Exposition.

Ben Reifel, who has his Ph.D. from Yale University, has served five terms in the U.S. House of Representatives as Congressman from South Dakota.

Another Indian who was an early graduate of Yale was Dr. Henry Roe Cloud who had his Doctor of Divinity degree from Emporia College. A Winnebago from the reservation in Nebraska, Dr. Cloud was a distinguished educator who founded an excellent school for Indians in Wichita and was later director of Indian education for the Bureau of Indian Affairs.

The first Indian woman physician was an Omaha. Dr. Susan La Flesche came from an unusual family. All of the five La Flesche children made their mark in the world. Francis, the only boy, was a noted anthropologist, and an older sister, Susette, was the first Indian woman spokesman on a national and international scale for the Indian people.

The La Flesche children were born in the period when tribal culture was beginning to vanish. Their father, Joseph, was the last recognized chief of the tribe and is mentioned in many histories of the west.

After receiving her medical degree from the Woman's Medical College of Philadelphia, Susan was appointed physician for the Omaha Reservation. She traveled on horseback day and night, in all kinds of weather, caring for 1300 Indians under the most primitive of conditions. There was no other doctor and no hospital.

One of the most famous names in this region of plains and mountains is that of Chief Joseph of the Nez Perce, one of the most remarkable of all Indians. The Nez Perce originally lived in Idaho and a part of Oregon and Washington. The Wallowa Valley, which they called "the valley of the winding waters," was traditionally theirs for centuries, and Old Joseph, the father of Chief Joseph, made his son promise that he would preserve it for his people.

In 1855, the Nez Perce ceded a large part of their land to the government and were given the Wallowa Valley in Oregon and a large part of Idaho. With the discovery of gold, the Oregon lands were immediately wanted and a new treaty was made which allowed the Indians only the Idaho lands.

Joseph and those who lived in the Valley refused to recognize the treaty but they were forced to move and some fighting took place from which erupted the first battle of the Nez Perce War.

Although Joseph had never been a warrior, he emerged as one of the greatest of Indian leaders and a military genius. He led his people on a 1,800-mile retreat lasting four months, in an attempt to reach the safety of Canada. Surrounded by armies on all sides, Joseph fought all the way. He had with him his women and children, his old, his sick, his wounded and dying. Yet he was able to outwit the armies and to bring his little band to within fifty miles of the Canadian border before he was cut off and made to surrender unconditionally. It was then that he spoke his often-quoted words: "From where the sun now stands, I will fight no more forever."

With his 450 followers, Joseph was taken to Indian Territory where many died from disease and the unused-to climate. Joseph pleaded that his people be allowed to return to their home, and finally they were sent to the Colville Reservation in Washington. A few descendants still live there, but the main body of the tribe is in Idaho.

Sacajawea, too, came from Idaho country. A Shoshone, she was captured by the Hidatsa when she was a girl in her teens and sold to Touissant Charbonneau, a French Canadian voyageur who made her his wife. With her husband, and carrying her newborn son on her back, she accompanied the Lewis and Clark expedition on their perilous journey to the Pacific coast, acting as guide and interpreter. Without Sacajawea, the success of the expedition might not have been possible, for she performed many valuable services. A number of statues and monuments have been erected to her memory throughout the West.

Chief Plenty Coups was a noted Crow Indian of modern times. He was head chief of his tribe from 1904 to 1932 and was one of the most widely known Indians of that period. Always a friend to white people, he worked through his active years to influence the Crows to advance in civilized ways and to seek economic independence.

He was a boy when he first went on the warpath and he earned his title of chief through a series of exploits which won him other war honors. At the time of the Custer Battle, he was a scout for the army and took part in a number of battles in which he had close calls with death.

Although the Montana settlers found Plenty Coups always willing to meet them more than halfway, at the same time he would not be imposed upon or pushed around. He became a farmer and stockman, recognizing the need to follow the "new trail," and plowed and cultivated his fields with his

41. 42. *Left:* Elderly Sioux in Plains costume. *Right:* Sioux Indian woman's costume made in the ancient tradition. The yoke was removed to work in warm weather.

43. Gros Ventre Indians with sacred medicine bundle which will be housed in a holy shrine.

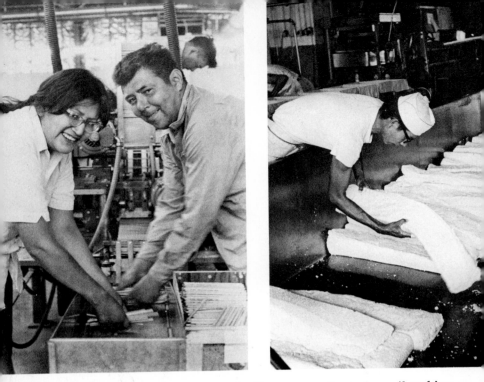

44. 45. *Left:* A husband and wife team work at a pencil-making factory on northern Montana's Blackfeet Reservation. *Right:* A Sioux worker at a cheese factory on Standing Rock Reservation in North Dakota cuts and cheddars cheese.

46. This Chippewa ski lodge on Rocky Boy's Reservation in Montana is an example of tribal enterprise in tourism.

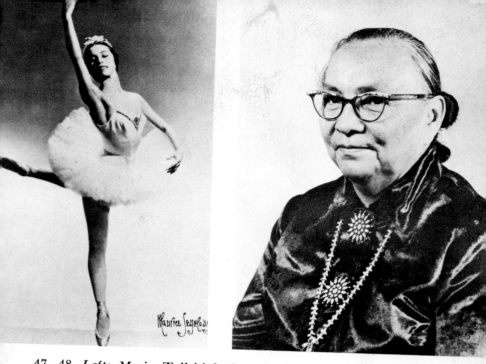

47. 48. *Left:* Maria Tallchief, Osage ballerina. *Right:* Annie Dodge Wauneka, Navajo health and welfare worker.

49. 50. *Left:* Susan La Flesche, an Omaha and the first Indian woman doctor. *Right:* Maria Martinez, potter of San Ildefonso.

51. 52. *Above:* Taos pueblo, one of the largest in the Southwest, located near Santa Fe, New Mexico. *Below:* Zuni Indians in western New Mexico use a "waffle bed" planting technique. The dried mud ridges retain the water during the growing season.

53. Indians of Santa Clara pueblo in New Mexico perform the ceremonial deer dance, a prayer for good hunting.

54. At Taos pueblo, New Mexico, an Indian examines beef drying on the roof.

55. Indians in willow and feather headdresses do the basket dance, a winter ceremonial at San Juan pueblo.

56. A number of Indian tribes used cradleboards. Children were carried in them on the mother's back or on the saddle of a horse. This is a Navajo child.

57. 58. The hogan (above) is typical of a Navajo home in use today. In contrast, Navajos (below) work as cutters and polishers at the diamond processing plant at Chandler, Arizona.

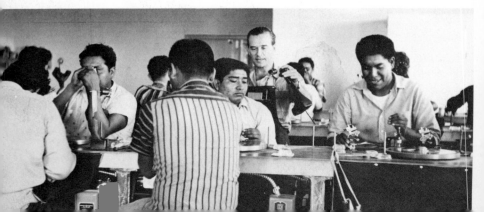

59. *Above:* Spinning wool into yarn which will be woven into Navajo blankets.

60. *Right:* Navajo mother and daughter working at the looms, weaving the famous Navajo blankets.

61. *Right:* Pomo basket of coiled willow, decorated with feathers and shell beads.

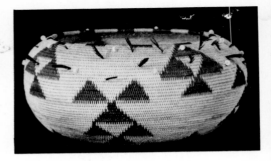

62. 63. *Left:* Earthenware jar, slip-painted, from the pueblo of Acoma. *Below:* A Zuni silver pin with inlays of shell and jet.

64. 65. *Below:* A Navajo blanket of wool (left) and a Hopi kachina doll of carved and painted cottonwood.

66. Painting of an Apache war party by Apache artist, Allan Houser, who is also noted for his sculpture.

67. Navajo Tribal Council house, Window Rock, Arizona. It is built of red sandstone in the shape of a huge hogan.

68. Apache dancer depicting the Apache Mountain Spirit Dance.

69. Statue representing Chief Solano, early leader of the Suisun tribe of California.

70. Housing development, Warm Springs Reservation, Oregon.

71. Authentic tipis, a feature of the Kah-nee-ta vacation resort on the Warm Springs Reservation.

72. A Quileute Indian sells his salmon catch at the dock.

73. Swinomish Indians haul in a trap net full of salmon.

74. One of two totem parks at Ketchikan, Alaska. It contains an authentic tribal house and totem poles from remote villages.

75. Replica of the house owned by Chief Shakes of the Tlingit Indians is at Wrangell, Alaska. Called Shark House, it was used for ceremonial dances and potlatches, and contained living quarters for the chief and resident families.

76. The Sun and Raven totem pole near Ketchikan, Alaska, tells the story of a great flood and how Raven helped man to survive.

77. Tlingit Indians from the village of Kake flank the world's tallest totem pole. Some are wearing the famous Chilkat blankets.

78. Tlingit dancers in typical costumes trimmed with pearl buttons

79. This unusual graveyard is in the village of Eklutna in Alaska. The brightly painted miniature houses are a strange combination of Indian designs and Russian Orthodox crosses.

80. General Ely S. Parker, Seneca chief and first Indian Commissioner of Indian Affairs.

81. Portrait of Pontiac, Ottawa chief, by John Mix Stanley

82. Bust of John Ross, principal chief of the Cherokee Nation

own hands. This was an unheard of thing for any Plains man to do. He was the first of the Crows to set out shade and fruit trees and to raise a garden. Before his death he gave part of his farm to the government for use as a park, with the provision that he would be buried there beside his wife.

The name of Plenty Coups is signed to practically every treaty or agreement made with the government by the Crows. He always appealed to the government that the Indians be treated fairly. Although his benefactions throughout his life to poorer Indians impoverished him in later years, he never sought personal help from the government.

In 1921 he was chosen to represent all Indians at the ceremonies at the tomb of the Unknown Soldier in Washington. He placed his war bonnet and coup stick on the grave as the last act of the impressive ceremonies, a gesture that could have no equal. When Plenty Coups died, the Crows abolished the title of chief, for they felt there could be no other person worthy of it.

The Kansa, or Kaw, Indians gave to the United States the only Indian Vice President. This was Charles Curtis, who was in office during the Hoover administration.

A small tribe, the Kansa were never very prominent in history. Mr. Curtis was a direct descendant of their chief, White Plume, and of Pawhuska, a chief of the Osage. He lived on the Kaw Reservation as a boy and at eight he became a jockey. When he gave up riding at sixteen, he was one of the leading jockeys of the central West. To finance his school expenses, he sold fruit at the railroad station and drove a hack at night. He began to study law when he was nineteen and was admitted to the bar, gaining recognition as a fine trial lawyer.

After serving as county attorney, he was elected to Congress in 1892, where he was the author of the Curtis Bill for the protection of the Indians of Indian Territory. He introduced much legislation favorable to Indians, in both House and Senate, among them a bill which gave them citizenship in 1924. His long and honorable career included fourteen years in the House and twenty years in the Senate where he was the Republican "whip." The speech he delivered to the Senate at the close of his term as Vice President is considered a classic.

Throughout the Plains and the mountain area there are evidences of both progressiveness and of deplorable living conditions. On the several Sioux reservations in the Dakotas, there is very great poverty. While some of the tribes have tribal assets, individual incomes are desperately low, housing is very bad, and employment is scarce. The land is poor and generally fitted only for grazing.

The Indians living on the Cheyenne River Reservation have been very successful, however, in starting a number of business enterprises, including a Super-value store, a garage and filling station, a laundromat, and a beef camp. The tribe, with assets of $24 million, also owns a profitable telephone franchise company.

On the Pine Ridge Reservation, the 11,000 Oglalas living there are at the other extreme. The reservation lands total a little less than three million acres, but only about 200 families engage in farming and a few in ranching. A moccasin factory gives some employment, but otherwise most are out of work, and the morale is very low. The Tribal Council is attempting to bring in industrial plants, but this is a long, slow process. Through its own efforts, the Council was able to secure funding for the construction of about 1,000 new housing units and it is attempting to make other improvements of the sad conditions.

The Flathead tribe is fortunate in having the large, scenic Flathead Lake on their Montana reservation and they operate a recreation facility on its shores and another at Hot Springs.

There is good electric power coming from the Kerr Dam which is located on land leased by the tribe and there are a number of excellent sites for the development of hydroelectric dams on the Flathead River.

The Flatheads are more self-sufficient than some tribes. They have a lively, progressive tribal government which has initiated a credit program so that members may borrow money to start businesses or improve homes or further their education.

The Northern Cheyennes have land that has produced a good income from stock grazing and now has a new potential. Oil companies have paid the tribe more than $1 million for leases, in addition to money paid for exploratory rentals. No oil has been found as yet but the promise is there. A major coal company has also been exploring for coal and a large deposit has been found under the rolling grassy river bottoms of the 415,000-acre reservation. In view of the present fuel crisis, large fuel companies are bidding for it as if it were gold.

Another large and valuable deposit exists on the adjacent Crow Reservation. However, many Indians on both reservations are opposing the exploitation of the coal fields. The Northern Cheyenne own the biggest chunk of the coal reserve—perhaps two million tons. While they see the prosperity that can come from the coal—at least $116,000 per individual—they see also thousands of whites moving in on the reservation and the doom of the Cheyenne way of life.

There are many people living in hard-core poverty on both reservations and the picture of wealth is a tempting one, even though it may hold the end of the two reservations and of the two tribal groups as tribes. With the mounting pressure for new sources of energy, the situation bids fair to become another explosive confrontation between Indians and the government which will stress "economic development" and "Indian self-determination."

On Wyoming's only reservation, the Shoshones and Arapahos living there have not as yet made effective use of their resources. Their lands are part of the best-watered area in Wyoming, with fertile valleys and rolling plains. The reservation comprises two million acres, and contains oil and gas. Most of the tribal income—about $3 million—comes from more than 300 oil wells and 39 gas wells. Other mineral resources are being explored. Yet these Indians lag far behind both economically and educationally.

A number of the tribes of the area are investing in tourism facilities. On the Fort Berthold Reservation in North Dakota the three affiliated tribes living there have built a $1.5 million motor lodge named for Four Bears, one of their famed chiefs. (Actually, there were two chiefs by the name of Four Bears, one a Mandan and the other an Hidatsa.)

Four Bears Lodge offers forty colorful, fully equipped units, a 24-unit trailer park, dining room, coffee shop, indoor heated pool, marina with rental and launch services, an airport, and an Indian museum on the shores of Lake Sakakawea. The complex is staffed almost entirely by Indians.

The Blackfeet Indians, living close to Glacier National Park in Montana, have also developed tourism facilities, historic trails, and other tourist attractions. There is also a pencil manufacturing plant on the reservation which is doing very well.

Although Oklahoma has more Indian tribes than any other state, it has only one reservation—the Osage. The Osages purchased their lands after selling their holdings in Missouri and Kansas. They wished to continue their hunting style of life, and so did not select an area more adaptable to farming, never thinking that hunting would not go on forever. Except for a strange quirk of fate, the tribe would have found themselves in serious difficulty. Instead, with the discovery of oil on their reservation, they became the wealthiest tribe in the country.

In 1920, an Osage family of five received $40,000 in payment of oil shares. No longer did the Osages ride horseback. They rode in cars—expensive Cadillacs, Pierce-Arrows, and Packards. Few knew how to drive, and so they had chauffeurs. Often they would abandon a car that was disabled, to buy a new one rather than have it repaired. No longer did they live in the Indian-style dwellings, but built fine houses and mansions, although an Indian house might be in the yard for the older people who preferred the traditional style of dwelling. The older people, too, clung to Indian clothing, although the women wore colorful imported shawls instead of blankets.

With so much money, the Osages were prey to all sorts of individuals with schemes for taking it away from them. Often their lives were in danger and they had to be placed under special protection. Today, though not quite as wealthy as they once were, the Osages have adjusted well to modern living. For most, the old ways are far behind them.

One of the best known of Oklahoma Indians is Maria Tallchief of the Osages. Acknowledged as one of the greatest ballerinas of all time—the only American dancer to achieve the status of prima ballerina—Miss Tallchief has danced in every corner of the globe and in almost every country of the world. Her sister Marjorie has also won considerable fame and is among the "greats" of the ballet stage.

When the Five Civilized Tribes were settled in Indian Territory, they purchased all of what is now Oklahoma except the Panhandle. The tribes attempted to pick up their lives again as they had been lived in the eastern woodlands. They established anew their own governments, complete in all phases, including executive, legislative, and judicial divisions, and each nation was treated as a separate political entity by the United States government. Each nation established its own capital—the Cherokees at Tahlequah, the Choctaws at Tahlihina, the Chickasaws at Tishomingo, the Creeks at Okmulgee, and the Seminoles at Wewoka. All of the capitol buildings are well preserved today except for the Seminole one.

Churches, schools, and towns were founded, land was cultivated, and cattle herds built up. The first institutions of free public education were the Cherokee male and female seminaries. The Creeks were instrumental in establishing Bacone College, for many years a school for Indians and a thriving integrated college today.

These days of reconstruction were not accomplished without considerable hardship, and they were not to last. With the outbreak of the Civil War, the Five Nations, who still had a great love for the South and who were southern in their sympathies, entered into an alliance with the Confederacy. Indian officers raised troops in each of the Nations. There were at least eleven Indian regiments, three battalions, three squadrons, a company, and a number of miscellaneous units. There were more than 11,000 enlisted Indians and all were outstanding in service, participating in nineteen battles and many skirmishes.

Throughout the war, the Cherokee, Stand Watie, proved to be a peerless leader. Colonel Watie was promoted to brigadier general and placed in command of the First Indian Cavalry Brigade. He was the only Indian of that rank in the Confederate Army. The Indian Nations of Indian Territory were the last in the Confederacy to surrender.

Indian country was laid waste, homes and fortunes were wrecked, and the cattle herds were stolen. With all others, Indians had to free their slaves. Even so, their lands were confiscated as punishment because of the Indians' loyalty to the South. The Five Tribes strongly protested this, for they had bought their lands with their own money. A compromise was finally worked out in which they were compelled to cede half of Indian Territory to be used for the settlement of various tribes from the Plains. They were also forced to grant citizenship to their former slaves and their descendants, and in some cases to allot them tribal land.

Once more, the Indians picked themselves up and reconstruction began. But just as it had been in the past, Indian lands became the mecca for white settlement, and finally much of western Oklahoma was opened to whites by lottery or land runs. In the various runs, settlers lined up around the borders of a designated territory and at a given signal, ran, rode, or walked to the area they wished to claim. Later, remaining land was alloted to various tribes or reserved for sale. This paved the way for the formation of the state of Oklahoma and its entry into the union in 1907.

With the coming of statehood, many Indians became outstanding leaders in Oklahoma, both in the state legislature and in the Congress of the United States. Many fundamentally sound laws from their own statute books had an extensive influence on Oklahoma legislation through the years and Indians served in the courts of the state. In recent times, Napoleon B. Johnson, a Cherokee, was Chief Justice of the Oklahoma Supreme Court.

Indian people contributed immeasurably to the cultural and spiritual life of the state as well as to its wealth and stability. It was the Choctaw people who gave the name of Oklahoma, in their language meaning "Red People." The Oklahoma state flag displays an Osage warrior's shield decorated with pendant eagle feathers, across its face an Indian pipe of peace crossed with an olive branch. The state seal is also strongly Indian in design. The seven-pointed star bearing a wreath of oak leaves is the symbol of the Cherokees; an upward ray depicts an Indian warrior with bow and shield taken from the ancient shield of the Chicakasaw; a tomahawk, a bow, and three crossed arrows is the emblem of the Choctaw; the Seminoles are represented by an Indian in a canoe, and a sheaf of wheat and a plow stand for the Creeks.

The affairs of the Five Tribes are administered by Tribal Chiefs, or governors, who were formerly appointed by the president of the United States but are now elected by the people. The Bureau of Indian Affairs maintains some supervision, even though there are no formal reservations.

Many of the old Plains leaders, especially from the Kiowa and Apache, are buried at Fort Sill, Oklahoma, in a cemetery known as the Indian Arlington. Geronimo lies there, as does Setanka, Quanah Parker, Kicking Bird, and others.

TRIBES OF THE PLAINS AND MOUNTAINS

(Colorado, Idaho, Kansas, Montana, Nebraska, North Dakota, South Dakota, Oklahoma, West Texas, Wyoming)

Akokisa	West Texas
Anadarko	West Texas
Apache ("enemy")	Oklahoma, West Texas
Jicarilla ("little basket")	
Lipan ("people")	
Aranama	West Texas, Oklahoma
Arapaho	Dakotas, Kansas, Oklahoma, Wyoming, Colorado
Arikara ("horn")	Dakotas, Montana
Atsina ("cut people")	Montana
Assiniboine ("cook by stones")	Dakotas, Montana, Canada
Bannock	Idaho, Wyoming
Bidai ("brushwood people")	West Texas
*Biloxi	Oklahoma
Blackfeet	· Montana, Canada
Kainah (Blood)	
Piegan	
Siksika (Blackfeet)	
*Caddo	Oklahoma
*Cherokee ("cave people")	Oklahoma, West Texas
Cheyenne ("speaks with alien tongue")	Dakotas, Kansas, Montana, Wyoming, Oklahoma
*Chickasaw	Oklahoma
Chippewa ("puckered")	North Dakota
*Choctaw	Oklahoma
Comanche	Kansas, Oklahoma, West Texas, Colorado, Wyoming
Cree	Montana, Canada
*Creek	Oklahoma

---

* An asterisk before a tribe means that the tribe was not native to the area but was a migrant, or a removed tribe.

Coeur d'Alene ("awl heart")	Idaho
Crow	Montana, Wyoming
Dakota (Sioux)	Dakotas, Montana, Wyoming, Nebraska

(Divisions) Teton
Santee
Sisseton
Yankton
Yanktonnai

(Bands) Brulé
Oglala
Hunkpapa
Wahpeton
Blackfoot
Minneconjou
Sans Arc
Two Kettle
Mdewakanton
Wahpekute

*Delaware	Oklahoma
Flathead (Salish)	Montana, Idaho
*Fox	Oklahoma
Gros Ventre ("big belly")	North Dakota
Guasco	West Texas
Hidatsa ("willows")	Dakotas
*Illinois ("men")	Kansas, Oklahoma
*Iowa ("sleepy ones")	Kansas, Oklahoma
Kalispel ("camas lily")	Montana, Idaho
Kansa (Kaw)	Kansas
Kichai ("going in wet sand")	Oklahoma, West Texas
*Kickapoo	Oklahoma
Kiowa ("principal people")	Oklahoma, Wyoming
Kiowa Apache	Nebraska, Oklahoma, Kansas
Kutenai (Kootenay)	Montana, Idaho
Mandan	North Dakota
*Miami	Oklahoma
*Micosuki	Oklahoma
*Missouri	Kansas, Oklahoma
*Munsee	Oklahoma

*Muskogee	Oklahoma
*Natchez	Oklahoma
Nez Perce ("pierced nose")	Idaho, Montana, Oklahoma
*Okmulgee	Oklahoma
Omaha ("going upstream")	Nebraska, Kansas
Osage	Missouri, Kansas, Oklahoma
Oto ("lechers")	Kansas, Oklahoma
*Ottawa ("traders")	Kansas, Oklahoma
Paiute	Idaho
Palouse	Idaho
Patiri	West Texas
Pawnee ("horn")	Nebraska, Kansas, Oklahoma, Wyoming
*Peoria	Oklahoma
*Ponca	Kansas, Oklahoma, Nebraska
*Potawatomi ("fire people")	Kansas, Oklahoma
*Quapaw	Kansas, Oklahoma
*Sauk (Sac)	Kansas, Oklahoma
Sematusa ("foolish ones")	Montana
*Seminole ("runaway")	Kansas, Oklahoma
*Seneca ("people of standing stone")	Kansas, Oklahoma
*Shawnee ("southerners")	Kansas, Oklahoma
Shoshone	Montana, Wyoming, Idaho
Sioux (See Dakota)	
Spokan	Idaho
Tigua	West Texas
Tonkawa	Oklahoma
Ute	Colorado
Wichita	Kansas, Oklahoma
*Winnebago ("filthy water")	Nebraska
*Wyandot (Huron)	Kansas, Oklahoma

Major Linguistic Stocks
Algonquian
Athapascan
Caddoan
Iroquoian
Kitunahan
Muskhogean
Salishan
Shahaptian
Siouan
Shoshonean
Tanoan
Tonkawan

INDIAN RESERVATIONS OF THE PLAINS AND MOUNTAINS

NORTH DAKOTA

Fort Berthold (Arikara, Mandan, Gros Ventre) — Dunn, McLean, Mercer, McKenzie, Mountrail counties

Devil's Lake (Fort Totten) (Sioux) — Ramsey county

Turtle Mountain (Chippewa) — Rolette county

Standing Rock (Sioux) — Sioux county

SOUTH DAKOTA

Cheyenne River (Sioux) — Dewey and Ziebach counties

Crow Creek (Sioux) — Buffalo and Hyde counties

Lower Brulé (Sioux) — Lyman county

Sisseton (Sioux) — Roberts county

Pine Ridge (Sioux) — Shannon and Washabaugh counties

Yankton (Sioux) — Charles Mix county

Rosebud (Sioux) — Todd county

Standing Rock (Sioux) — Corson county

NEBRASKA

Omaha-Winnebago — Thurston county

Santee (Ponca, Sioux) — Knox county

MONTANA

Fort Peck (Assiniboine, Sioux) — Roosevelt county

Fort Belknap (Assiniboine, Gros Ventre) — Blaine county

Rocky Boy's (Chippewa, Cree) — Hill and Chouteau counties

Blackfeet — Glacier county

Crow — Big Horn and Yellowstone counties

Tongue River (Northern Cheyenne) — Big Horn and Rosebud counties

Flathead (Salish, Kutenai) — Lake county

WYOMING

Wind River (Shoshone, Arapaho) — Fremont county

COLORADO
Southern Ute   Montezuma county
Ute Mountain   Montezuma county

OKLAHOMA
Osage   Osage county

IDAHO
Fort Hall (Shoshone, Bannock)   Bingham and Power
                                                   counties
Nez Perce   Nez Perce county
Coeur d'Alene   Benewah county
Western Shoshone (Shoshone, Paiute)   Owyhee county
Kootenai   Boundary county

Non-reservation Communities

TEXAS
Tigua   Bexar county

KANSAS
Sac and Fox, Iowa   Brown county (Kansas)
                                                   and Richardson county
                                                   (Nebraska)
Kickapoo   Brown county
Potawatomi   Jackson county

OKLAHOMA
Apache   Comanche county
Arapaho   Custer county
Caddo   Comanche county
Cherokee   Cherokee, Sequoyah, Mus-
                                                   kogee, Wagoner coun-
                                                   ties
Cheyenne   Custer county
Chickasaw   Johnston, Atoka, Bryan
                                                   counties
Choctaw   Pittsburg, Latimer, Has-
                                                   kell, Pushmataha, Le
                                                   Flore, Choctaw counties
Comanche   Comanche county

Creek	Creek, Okmulgee, McIntosh, Okfuskee counties
Delaware	Ottawa county
Iowa	Pottawatomie county
Kaskaskia (Illinois)	Ottawa county
Kaw	Kay county
Kickapoo	Pottawatomie county
Kiowa	Caddo county
Miami	Ottawa county
Modoc	Ottawa county
Oto	Pawnee county
Ottawa	Ottawa county
Pawnee	Pawnee county
Peoria	Ottawa county
Ponca	Pawnee county
Potawatomi	Pottawatomie county
Quapaw	Ottawa county
Sac and Fox	Pawnee county
Seminole	Seminole county
Seneca	Ottawa county
Shawnee	Pawnee county
Tonkawa	Kay county
Wea	Ottawa county
Wichita	Caddo county
Wyandot	Ottawa county

Indians of the Southwest

Thousands of years before the Southwest country was occupied by today's Indians, there were people living in the cliffs known as Cliff Dwellers. Ruins of the cliff dwellings are seen today throughout Arizona, New Mexico, Colorado, and Utah. Some of the houses were made of masonry and others were dug into the cliffs which formed natural fortresses. No one knows how old the cliff dwellings are. This can only be guessed at. They may go back to prehistoric times.

It is believed that the Cliff Dwellers were, in the main, the ancestors of the Pueblo Indians. They were agricultural, but sought to live in the cliffs as a protection from warlike tribes who were raiders. Their dwellings were in remote canyon walls and on the edges of barren and almost inaccessible plateaus, built at enormous cost in time and labor. Some rooms were merely storage places for corn and other supplies, while others had watch towers from which the fields could be watched and the coming of strangers noted.

The Indians living in the Southwest are considerably different from those of the Plains in their way of life. The major culture was a sedentary agricultural one, marked by the Pueblo Indians whose adobe houses were like apartment buildings. These settlements were given the name of *pueblo*, or town, by the Spaniards.

With a few other native groups, the Pueblos were a peaceful people and remarkable farmers. Some understood and developed irrigation from prehistoric times. Others were dry farmers, depending upon the mysterious swelling and sinking of the Colorado River to provide water for their crops.

The Hopi are also Pueblo Indians. There is little difference between the two groups, except that in Arizona they are called Hopi and in New Mexico, Pueblo. These Indians raised fine crops of a number of kinds of corn and beans, squashes and pumpkins. They raised a wild cotton plant from which they wove cloth, and they domesticated the wild turkey. They did little hunting, except for small game.

The Pueblo Indians were the only ones of the desert tribes living in adobe buildings. All have lived in the arid country most successfully for centuries. Basketry and pottery making was developed to a high level of artistic creation and each group had its own distinctive and recognizable styles and designs.

Unlike other tribes which considered planting and growing the work of women because it was concerned with creation, the Pueblo men were the farmers. The gardens were usually some distance from the villages, built on mesa tops for protective reasons, and so they had to be good runners. They ran back and forth to the fields each day.

In later years, Louis Tewanima, a Hopi, was selected for the U.S. Olympic team of 1912 without undergoing trials. He had previously been on the 1908 Olympic team, where he ran ninth in the marathon. On the 1912 team he placed second in the 10,000-meter run. No American bettered his time at that distance until the 1964 Tokyo Games when the record was shattered by Billy Mills, a Sioux Indian. When he was inducted into the Arizona Hall of Fame in 1957, Tewanima told of how he used to run down rabbits as a child, and that he would sometimes run to Winslow, a 120-mile round trip, just to watch the trains go by.

The Pueblo men, rather than the women, were also the weavers, while the women built the homes and owned all of the property related to them. There was much elaborate ritual and ceremony, with both men and women participating, and ceremonies were usually prayers for rain. One of the most noted is the Snake Dance, usually held by the Hopi Indians in August.

Many of the ceremonies centered around the *kachinas*, spirit beings of great power supposedly living in the San Francisco peaks. In every Peublo household there are carved figures representing these spirits which are given to the children, not as playthings, but to teach them about the kachinas and to be revered as household gods. There are very many kachinas, some 250 at least. In some of the dances, men representing the kachinas wear carved and painted masks symbolical of the particular spirit.

The nomadic Apaches and Navajos were latecomers to the Southwest region and it is believed that they came from the far north. Both groups had many aspects of the life-style of the Plains, but they also took on much of the desert culture.

The Apaches, one of the best known of the southwestern tribes, gained their fame through their warlike dispositions. Traditionally nomadic warrior-raiders, they were seldom long enough in one place to bother with raising crops, making pottery or basketry, or having possessions. Their houses were rude shelters covered with coarse grass called *wickiups*.

Actually a grouping of several tribes, the Apaches were called "enemy" by their neighbors, but their own name for themselves, Diné, meant "people." The Apaches raided Indian and white settlements alike. Trappers and traders were the first Americans to come among them and, since they came alone or in pairs, they were not at first considered a danger by the Indians, who looked upon them with curiosity—and horror because of their bearded faces. Later, when larger parties began to show up, there was resentment. Treaties and agreements were made but usually broken, and this eventually led to bitter warfare. Troops were sent into the area to protect the incoming settlers, and forty years of fighting followed.

Some of the Apaches joined the Army as scouts. They were very valuable in all of the important campaigns, saving lives, money, and time in bringing the war with their tribesmen to an end. The Apaches were the last of the fighting tribes to end the struggle of Indian against white and to go onto the reservations. The early leaders are legendary today. Cochise, Geronimo, Mangas Coloradas, Victorio—all proud and brave men who asked no favors. They fought against overwhelming odds and when the end came, they accepted it as good losers.

Cochise was head of the Chiricahua Apaches. Though a skilled warrior, he was basically a peaceful man. He was on friendly terms with the American settlers and often traded with them, and he was generally admired and liked.

When it was first proposed that the Apaches move onto a reservation, Cochise steadfastly refused. Then he was falsely accused of kidnapping a white child. With some of his band, he appeared at the Army camp under a flag of truce to establish his innocence. However, five of his men were seized and hanged. The badly wounded Cochise fought like a wildcat to gain his freedom. From then on, he defied the soldiers for eleven years.

During the Civil War there was a pause in Indian-white hostilities. After the war, the Army renewed its efforts against the Apaches. Cochise offered to sign a peace treaty if his people would be allowed to keep the mountain lands as their home. This was promised, but the government refused to honor the promise and ordered the Chiricahuas to move to a reservation immediately.

Cochise's answer was continued warfare. From a mountain stronghold in southeastern Arizona, he attacked fifty-four times and killed and captured many whites. He finally surrendered and went to live on the San Carlos Reservation, living out his days peacefully.

About that same time, Geronimo began his continual raiding forays. At last he was captured and taken in chains to Fort Apache, but through some confusion, he was set free. When the Chiricahuas agreed to live on the reservation, Geronimo, like Cochise, refused to do so. He continued to raid the settlements for another ten years before he decided to go with his band to San Carlos. In a short time, he fled the reservation to lead another raiding party. Many lives were lost before he was once more captured, and this time he managed to escape. When finally captured again, he and those who fought with him were deported as prisoners to Florida. As the train carrying the Indians pulled out, the Army band played "Auld Lang Syne."

After a number of years, Geronimo and the other Apache prisoners were sent to Fort Sill in Oklahoma. There he became a prosperous farmer and was looked upon as a gentle person with a good sense of humor. He was a great friend of President Theodore Roosevelt.

The Apaches today are exceedingly progressive. The Jicarillas are worth over $10 million. They have natural gas and oil wells and one of New Mexico's largest untapped sources of underground water. The tribe owns an electronic manufacturing plant and has invested money in motion picture production. They have a $1 million scholarship fund available for their young people who wish to enter college.

All of the Apache groups have gone into tourism projects, the White Mountain Apaches perhaps more so than any

other. The White Mountain Recreational Enterprises over-
sees more than one-half of Arizona's clear streams with some
400 originating on their reservation. These teem with various
kinds of trout and the tribe has received the U.S. Department of Interior's Conservation Award for its work in pre-
serving the native Apache trout.

On the reservation, twenty-six recreational lakes and liter-
ally hundreds of smaller ponds have been created, and a
continuous stocking program keeps all waters alive with fish.
There are more than 1,000 camp sites and a year-round resort
complex has a 6,800-foot chairlift and miles of ski runs. There
are good roads, modern motels, cabins, boat rentals, marinas,
gas stations, grocery and sporting goods stores, and hundreds
of cabin sites for lease. Hunting is also open to outsiders on
the reservation. For people who were once so elusive and
wary, the Apaches have gone all out to make the tourist feel
welcome and at home among them.

The White Mountain group also owns a multimillion dol-
lar sawmill which was the first in the country to employ an
all-Indian crew. If the annual timber output were cut to 2 x 4
lumber and laid end to end it would encircle the globe with
enough left over to reach from the reservation to the equator!
The tribe realizes more than $5 million in profits from this
lumber business yearly.

The Apaches also own some of the finest beef stock in the
country. A herd of 20,000 white-faced herefords was developed from early days when the government promised to provide the Indians meat if they would settle on reservations.
The meat was delivered "on the hoof" to keep it from spoil-
ing, and a few far-seeing Apaches decided that it might be
more advantageous to raise the meat than to eat it. As the
herd grew in size, the Indians began to sell beef to the military, and gradually established a business that attracts more

than 200 buyers from over the country for the annual auctions.

Although the Apaches are entirely modern in their outlook on life, they retain a great deal of "Indianness." One of their well-known ceremonies is the Mountain Spirit Dance. (This is also called the Crown or Devil Dance.) The Mountain Spirits figure in some of the traditional rituals, especially the one that is held when a girl reaches the age of young womanhood. They appear after dark and disappear before dawn. No one knows who they are. They wear buckskin skirts and high boots ringed with bells and rattles. On their heads are great "crowns" of wood, painted or formed from carved symbolic designs. Their faces are completely covered by black cloth.

The dancers are accompanied and led by the Devil, who acts like a clown while the dancers make strange cries and go through precise, particular, and rhythmic routines around a blazing fire of large proportion. The singers chant and beat time by pounding on a dry cowhide with sticks. When they stop for breath, the dancers glide swiftly into the darkness away from the firelight.

Dr. Carlos Montezuma was an Apache who practiced medicine for many years in Chicago. Stolen when he was a child by the Pimas, he was sold to a traveling photographer who raised him as his son. Dr. Montezuma had a distinguished medical career and he was an inspiring spokesman for his people, his constant plea being to let them think and act for themselves.

The Hopi Indians have remained strongly traditional and they are a deeply religious people. They abide by their ancient ceremonies and adhere to the old way of life to a greater degree than some of their Pueblo relations. The Snake Dance, held in August, is a most important ceremony, for it is a prayer for rain. Non-Indians are permitted to attend, but pictures may not be taken. Throughout the ritual, the dancers carry live snakes which have been gathered from the desert and which are released when the ceremony is over so that they may carry the prayers of the people to the proper spirits.

The Hopi have not sought fame and fortune in the white man's world, nor have they encouraged their young people to do so. The best-known Hopi of today is Fred Kabotie, an outstanding artist who has been honored here and by the French government. Fred has remained close to his people and has helped them establish a silver guild which produces high-quality silver jewelry incorporating ancient Hopi designs.

In spite of the strictness of the traditionalists, modernism has not been entirely ruled out. Like others of the Pueblos, the Hopi are suspended between a timeless Indian world with its own beliefs and customs and the beckoning world of the white man, so deeply contrasting and so contradictory to the teachings of the past. The Hopi want to remain Indian but they cannot completely isolate themselves from the life going on around them. Younger generations will more and more grow away from the teachings of the elders.

The tribe has built a $900,000 center which is a tourism complex with a 33-unit motel, restaurant, museum, and craft shop. They have invested a half million dollars in a garment factory employing 200 Indians, and they are building new homes which have three bedrooms, a kitchen, and air-conditioning. They have established a center for the care of retarded children. Their woodworking industry furnishes the government with desk letter boxes, racks for coats and display, blackboards, and other items. The Hopi also share large coal reserves with the Navajo whose vast reservation encloses theirs like a box within a box.

When the Spaniards came into the Southwest, they brought with them sheep and goats, horses, peach trees, and other plants, which were good for the Indian people. But they also brought a harsh and severe rule and much suffering. They demanded complete obedience to Spanish laws, took what they wished, and killed if they were resisted. They insisted on conversion to the Church, and their impact upon the peaceful people was a heavy one.

As Spanish colonization and dominance grew, the Pueblo of Acoma revolted. Acoma is called the "sky city." Built upon a high mesa top, it is said to be the oldest continuously inhabited village in America. Indian bows and arrows were of little use against metal armor and stronger weapons, so there was little chance for the Acoma Indians. The Spaniards killed off the men and made slaves of the women and children. A few young men, held as captives, were also enslaved. Each had a foot cut off as punishment. Children under twelve were given to the priests. Perhaps some were sent to Spain.

After fifty years of this kind of bondage, the Pueblos joined with the Apaches in another losing fight with the Spaniards. Twenty years later another attempt against the Spanish was made and lost. Among those taking part was a man from the San Juan pueblo named Popé. Imprisoned, he went to Taos after his release, and organized another rebellion from the shelter of that isolated town.

All of the pueblos except Isleta now united under Popé, and nearly one-fifth of the Spaniards were wiped out. The rest fled to Texas. In the great victory celebration that was held, everything Spanish was burned or destroyed. Carried away by his success, Popé soon became a dictator, the equal of any Spaniard. The people rebelled against him and he was deposed but was later restored to power. When he died, the Spaniards once more tried to re-establish themselves. After four years of bitter fighting, they returned to Pueblo country. The ancient towns were rebuilt and the Pueblos never again went to war. But neither did they submit. Peaceful as they were, they were not meek, and they refused to give up any of their beliefs or to change their lives. The two peoples settled down to a harmonious arrangement. There were Spanish churches in every Pueblo, and many of the Indians became converts. At the same time, the Indian ceremonies went on as usual, the priests tolerating them and even permitting them to be a part of church services. At Christmas time, the Pueblos hold certain ceremonies which blend both Christian and Indian rituals.

Of the various pueblos, Zuni was the first to be visited by the Spaniards. It is also the first of the pueblos to accept full responsibility for running its affairs without the direct supervision of the Bureau of Indian Affairs. After years of conservatism, the Zunis have come suddenly to life and have completed an industrial park and an airstrip, and have two small industries already located on the reservation. A Housing Authority has completed a number of single dwelling units, which the Zunis refused to accept for at least three years because such houses were not in keeping with their pattern of extended family dwellings. The younger people liked the houses, however, and it is expected that a total of 850 will eventually be completed. The most productive industry is silversmithing and with some of the Zunis, this is a full-time occupation. Silversmithing brings in an income to the tribe in excess of $1 million.

The Indians at Isleta pueblo own and operate a pickle factory, but others of the pueblos have been slow to take on too much modernizing, although the young people find gainful employment in the towns and cities. Pottery is made at all of the pueblos, though not as much as formerly.

To speak of pottery is to speak of Maria Montoya Martinez from the pueblo of San Ildefonso. Maria's story typifies the togetherness and the spirit of sharing of the Pueblo people, who think it wrong to rise individually above one another. All are equal.

Maria Martinez is known the world over for her beautiful pottery which she revived from an ancient method. She had always made pottery, but she became intensely interested when she was shown some shards of a black lustre ware that none of the Indians knew how to make or anything about. The shards had been found by archeologists digging into ancient ruins. With her husband Julian, Maria experimented for months trying to find the method used in making this old pottery. At last, purely by chance, she discovered the secret and a new art form was born.

More months of experimentation were needed to find a way to decorate the pottery with a fluid that comes out of the firing as a dull etched effect against the high lustre of the black ware. When all was perfected, Maria developed her art into an industry from which the entire community of San Ildefonso profited, earning more through such sales than from their farm products.

Maria taught the women of San Ildefonso to make the new pottery, insisting only that each piece be of excellent workmanship. Julian taught the men how to apply the decoration, and only the old designs were used. From the beginning, Maria's pieces won many prizes, but after three successive years of prize-winning, she refused to accept any more. She wanted the other women to have the encouragement of such recognition. Her beautiful pottery is found in every major museum in this country and in many European ones. Now in her eighties, Maria seldom makes pottery these days. But she can look back to a lifetime of service to her people and of sharing with them something that came from her own creativeness and that brought them such good.

The Navajo tribe, now the largest in the country, is, like the Apache, not native to the Southwest, coming there by way of some long-ago migration from the far north. When the Navajos arrived, they preferred to live as wanderers, hunting and raiding. They did not live in villages and did not have chiefs. Related families might cluster together under the leadership of a "headman."

By the time the Spaniards arrived, the Navajo had become more settled. They had begun to farm, and they had learned weaving from the Hopi and Pueblo women whom they captured. They did not make baskets or pottery.

Somehow, they obtained horses and sheep from the Spaniards and these two animals were to change them completely and bring them undreamed-of wealth. With their flocks of sheep, they always had meat and wool for weaving blankets and dresses. A loom could be set up anywhere, so that weaving was an ideal craft for a people who still moved about, taking their flocks from pasture to pasture. Horses gave them a swift mobility and they could travel miles in a day, swooping down on some village, taking what was wanted, and galloping away to strike some place else.

The women owned the sheep and the men owned the horses. With sheepskins and weavings to trade, and horses and captives to sell as slaves, the people grew strong and rich. They were no longer drifters with nothing of their own. They were established herders and shepherds—people of property—the only shepherd Indians without villages in all America.

The Navajos were unique in all that they did. Where they copied from others, they improved what they copied. They adopted and adapted all that seemed good and that would be useful to them, making it over in a way that was theirs alone.

When the Americans came into the Southwest, smaller tribes begged them for protection from the Navajos, who continued to prey upon them. Since there were no Navajo chiefs, there was no one with whom peace treaties could be

negotiated. At last, with matters at their worst, Kit Carson
was sent to remove the tribe to Fort Sumner. As soon as the
soldiers appeared, the Navajos disappeared. Carson destroyed their fields and their peach orchards, and starved the
people into submission. They had no choice other than to
do what he said.

The 300-mile journey to Fort Sumner is called the "long
walk" by the Navajos, for they walked every step of the way.
There were a few wagons but these were for the old, the sick,
and the very young. At the fort, no preparations had been
made for them. They were given only flour, coffee beans, and
now and again a slab of tough bacon—and they did not know
how to use any of these things. There were no shelters of any
kind, not even brush ones, so the people slept in pits in the
ground. There was no firewood. Clothes were made from
flour sacks. Seeds that were given them were planted, but
the crops were destroyed by worms or killed by drought.

The government talked of sending the miserable people to
Oklahoma, but the Navajos begged to go home. They promised they would never raid again, and they kept their promise,
even though they were sent home with nothing. As hungry
as they were, they did not try to get food from other people.

After several months of extreme suffering, the government
brought in sheep and goats and every family was given
enough to start a flock again. Gradually, they found their
way back to better living. A sheep industry was started which
would be worth many thousands of dollars in later years, and
they would have a herd of more than 100,000 horses.

Now the white trader and the railroad came, and the people could exchange sacks of wool and sheepskins for the
things in the trader's store. The women became such expert
weavers that their work ranks among the finest in the world.
The men learned to make silver jewelry from hammered-
down American silver dollars and Mexican pesos and the

blue turquoise so plentiful in the region. They, too, became expert in this form of art which spread to the Pueblo and the Hopi, each having its own way of doing it. Every Navajo and his horse was hung with silver and turquoise jewelry and the handmade pieces became another source of revenue. Today, with its acceptance as "high fashion," Indian jewelry is commanding high prices.

Until about twenty-five years ago, the Navajo clung to their own way of life. Now they are very much a part of the twentieth century, a proud, enterprising people, taking and adapting from the white economy, yet retaining a distinctive Navajo identity.

Fifty years ago, for the first time in Navajo history, a Tribal Council was elected, with a chairman and with administrative powers. The Council initiated many progressive steps. They made certain that all Navajo children attended school and established a $10,000,000 perpetual scholarship fund for their young people for higher education. They built a sawmill and began a lumber industry, opened an agricultural school with a course in irrigation farming, invited industries to locate on the reservation or nearby, opened their own supermarket, constructed their own airport, built several fine motels and a tribal museum, established their own newspaper and their own college. Recently they opened a training course in optics, and other enterprises are on the planning board. The tribal income is so large that modern sophisticated computers are used for bookkeeping.

One of the most famous Indian women in America comes from the Navajo tribe. Mrs. Annie Dodge Wauneka is the daughter of Henry Chee Dodge, the first tribal chairman and a highly respected leader. The first woman to be elected to the Tribal Council, Mrs. Wauneka heads the committee on health and welfare. A human dynamo, she has been honored many times, for she has done much to improve the health conditions of her people. In 1963, she was one of thirty-one Americans singled out to receive the presidential Medal of Freedom from President John F. Kennedy. A tall, dignified person, dressed always in Navajo dress, Mrs. Wauneka commands attention as few people do wherever she goes.

The Pima Indians in Arizona, too, are fighting their way up from grinding poverty under which they have lived for many years. A lack of education and training has hindered them in getting employment adjacent to the reservation. On the reservation, there is no work, although some cotton is raised.

With the help of various federal agencies and the Bureau of Indian Affairs, the Tribal Council planned what they call the "reservation bootstrap operation." The plan includes some fifty-one projects. The immediate major goals are now being met and most projects are proceeding on schedule. The most dramatic effect was to raise permanent employment from 25 per cent to 45 per cent and to increase the average family income per year.

The core of the economic development phase is the completion of three industrial parks and the establishment of a Small Business Administration Center in the reservation agency town of Sacaton. One of the industrial parks is to be allocated for agricultural use.

For the Allis-Chalmers Company, the tribe constructed a headquarters building for a heavy equipment test site and leased 5,400 acres of reservation land for mineral exploration. A reservation-wide park system will include a state park, two roadside parks, and four other parks, all to be constructed by the tribe. A community recreational building and Youth Rehabilitation Center have been completed. Other projects have to do with water conservation and the development of water systems, housing improvements, an agricultural cooperative, a national monument, a cooperative game management program, and an air training facility. A Career Guidance unit has been established which provides vocational counseling. The Pimas are well on their way to a better life for the entire tribe.

Papago Indians provided the land for the construction of the Kitt Peak National Observatory where the world's largest telescope is to be set. Kitt Peak is sacred to the Papago, but they cooperated willingly in making this important scientific development possible, requesting only that the area be maintained free from litter and protected from careless tourists and picnickers.

Of all the tribes of America, with the exception of Alaska, the Havasupai are the most remote. For the past nine centuries they have lived in an isolated inner gorge at the bottom of the Grand Canyon.

Although they have remained withdrawn from the outside world, time has not passed them by. The old willow brush and red sandstone houses are about gone and no more do the people sleep on earthen floors. Modern pre-fab houses, brought in by helicopter, are becoming the way of life. There are electric stoves and refrigerators. Food is no longer dried for winter use, there is no more piñon seed gathering, and the rabbit drives, which were a hunt as well as a sport, are all part of the past. But some age-old customs and rituals still exist.

To arrive at the village means travel by horse over a rugged eight-mile trail down the canyon side. The Supai village is the only one in the United States that sends and receives mail and supplies by pack train. There is a small school, but the children from fourth grade on are sent away to government boarding schools. Movies are shown, and the people prefer westerns to any other kind. The children yell as loud when the cowboys chase the Indians as do children anywhere else. Once in a while they may ask when the Indians are going to win, but mostly the fact of white against Indian makes no impression. Existence is tranquil and easy, and the cares of the world at large are far away.

The southwestern Indians have become noted as fire fighters since the Bureau of Indian Affairs trained a fire-fighting crew of Mescalero Apaches in 1948. Since then, 25-member units have been formed by Hopi, Papago, and Navajo, and a number of the Pueblos. The fire-fighting Indians have gained such renown that other units have been formed among northern tribes. The highly trained Indians are sent for when major forest fires are raging in any part of the West. They perform a vital service for the nation and take great pride in their work and in themselves. They know they will be sent to the roughest country or to where the fire is the most difficult to control—and they know they will be treated with the greatest respect.

TRIBES OF THE SOUTHWEST

(Arizona, New Mexico, Southern California, Nevada, Utah, Southern Colorado)

Apache ("enemy")
  Chiricahua
  Lipan ("people")
  Jicarilla ("little basket")
  Mescalero ("mescal people")
  San Carlos
  White Mountain
  Tonto
	Arizona, New Mexico

Chemeheuvi	Arizona, Southern California
Cocopah	Arizona
Gosiute (Goshute)	Utah, Nevada
Havasupai ("blue water people")	Arizona
Hopi ("peaceful ones")	Arizona

(Towns)

Hotevilla	Shungopovi
Kisakobi	Polacca
Moenkapi	Jeddito
Shipaulovi	Mishongnovi
Walpi	Second Mesa
Homolobi	Sichomovi
Kuchaptuvela	Tonalea
Oraibi	

Manso	New Mexico
Maricopa	Arizona
Mohave ("three mountains")	Arizona, Southern California
Navajo ("great planted fields")	Arizona, New Mexico, Southern Utah, Southern Colorado
Paiute ("true Ute")	Arizona, Utah, Nevada
Papago ("bean people")	Arizona
Pecos	New Mexico
Pima ("I don't know")	Arizona

Pueblo — New Mexico
  Jemez (pueblo: Jemez)
  Zuni (pueblo: Zuni)
  Keres (pueblos: Acoma, Cochiti, Laguna, San Felipe, Santa Ana, Santo Domingo, Zia)
  Tewa (pueblos: Pojoaque, Nambe, San Ildefonso, Santa Clara, Tesuque, San Juan)
  Tiwa (pueblos: Isleta, Picuris, Sandia, Taos)
Quahitika — Arizona
Shoshone — Nevada, Utah
Ute — Utah, New Mexico, Southern Colorado

Walapai (Hualapai) ("pine tree people") — Arizona, Southern California

Washoe — Nevada
Yavapai ("sun people") — Arizona
Yuma — Arizona, Southern California

Major Linguistic Stocks
Athapascan
Shoshonean
Yuman
Tanoan
Keresan
Piman
Zunian
Washoan

INDIAN RESERVATIONS IN THE SOUTHWEST

ARIZONA

Ak-Chin (Maricopa)	Pinal county
Colorado River (Chemehuevi, Mohave, Hopi, Navajo)	Yuma county (Arizona), Riverside and San Bernardino counties (California)
Cocopah	Yuma county
Fort Mohave	Mohave county (Arizona), San Bernardino county (California), Clark county (Nevada)
Fort Yuma	Yuma county (Arizona), Imperial county (California)
Fort Apache	Apache, Navajo, Gila counties
Hopi	Navajo, Coconino counties
Kaibab (Paiute)	Mohave, Coconino counties
Gila Bend (Papago)	Maricopa county
San Xavier (Papago)	Pima county
Papago	Pima, Pinal, Maricopa counties
Gila River (Pima, Maricopa)	Maricopa, Pinal counties
Fort McDowell (Yavapai)	Pinal county
Salt River (Pima)	Maricopa county
San Carlos (Apache)	Gila, Graham, Pinal counties
Hualapai	Coconino, Mohave, Yavapai counties
Havasupai	Coconino county
Yavapai	Yavapai county
Camp Verde (Yavapai)	Yavapai county
Navajo	Navajo, Apache, Coconino counties (Arizona), San Juan county (New Mexico), La Plata county (Colorado), Washington county (Utah)

Alamo (Navajo)	Socorro county
Canoncito (Navajo)	Bernalillo county
Jicarilla (Apache)	Rio Arriba county
Mescalero (Apache)	Otero county
Pueblo	Bernalillo, Torrance, Taos, Santa Fe, Sandoval, Valencia, McKinley counties
Puertocito (Navajo)	Socorro county

NEVADA

Battle Mountain (Shoshone)	Lander county
Carson Colony (Washoe)	Lyon county
Dresslerville Colony (Washoe)	Douglas county
Duck Valley (Shoshone-Paiute)	Elko county (Nevada), Owyhee county (Idaho)
Duckwater (Shoshone)	Nye county
Elko Colony (Shoshone)	Elko county
Ely Colony (Shoshone)	White Pine county
Fallon Colony (Paiute)	Churchill county
Fort McDermitt (Paiute, Shoshone)	Humboldt county (Nevada), Malheur county (Oregon)
Goshute (Goshute-Shoshone)	White Pine county (Nevada), Juab, Tooele counties (Utah)
Las Vegas Colony (Paiute)	Clark county
Lovelock (Paiute)	Pershing county
Moapa (Paiute)	Clark county
Odgers Ranch (Shoshone)	Elko county
Pyramid Lake (Paiute)	Washoe county
Reno-Sparks Colony (Paiute-Washoe)	Washoe county
Ruby Valley	Elko county
South Fork (Te-Moak)	Elko county
Summit Lake (Paiute)	Humboldt county
Walker River (Paiute-Shoshone)	Churchill, Lyon, Mineral counties
Washoe Ranches	Douglas county
Winnemucca Colony (Shoshone)	Humboldt county

Yerington Colony (Paiute)   Lyon county
Yerington (Campbell Ranch) (Paiute) Lyon county
Yomba (Shoshone)   Nye county

UTAH

Uintah-Ouray (Ute)   Uintah, Duchesne, Grand,
                                       Wasatch counties

Skull Valley (Goshute-Shoshone)   Tooele county

SOUTHERN COLORADO

Southern Ute   La Plata county
Ute Mountain (Ute)   Montezuma county

Non-reservation Communities

UTAH

Cedar City (Paiute)   Iron county
Indian Peaks (Paiute)   Beaver county
Kanosh (Paiute)   Millard county
Koosharem (Paiute-Ute)   Sevier county
Shivwitz (Paiute)   Washington county

Indians of California

California Indian tribes are the least known of all those in the country, yet the area was one of the most densely populated in the United States. Although they were early in contact with the Spaniards, many of them did not come to light, or their names had not been heard of, as late as the 1840's when the gold rush began in the state.

There were some forty major tribes in the region and about 500 very small groups or bands. They belonged to the greatest number of linguistic stocks and all but three were native to California.

Although they were somewhat unsettled and moved about as the various wild foods ripened, they were never a nomadic people, nor were they warlike. In the southern and central part of the area, the Indians lived very simply. They were not hunters or farmers, except for those on the Arizona border, but gatherers of seeds, roots, fruits, and berries, and especially of acorns, the staple article of food. These were ground into a meal and then filtered many times with water in a basket so tightly woven that the flour was not lost but the poisonous juice of the acorn was leached out.

Basket making was the great craft and all of the California Indian baskets were marvels of exquisite design and construction. Some were woven so tightly that they could be used as cooking vessels, and some were interwoven with colored feathers and, later, with beads when these were obtained from traders. Pottery making was not well established, for little, if any, was made.

The southern Indians lived in reed or brush shelters, but in the north the Indians built permanent homes of planks cut from redwood trees. Although the northerners did some gathering of wild foods, they were mainly hunters and fishermen. Several tribes lived on the islands off the southern coast and shared with their cousins, the Chumash, a coastal tribe, the uniqueness of being the only Indians of the continent to build plank canoes.

The Spaniards first visited California in 1542, but there was no colonization until 1769 when the first of the Spanish missions was built at San Diego. Twenty others followed, between there and a little to the north of San Francisco.

The Indians did not resist the Spaniards and were persuaded to become converts of the Church and to settle around the missions where they would be cared for as children by the padres, who would watch over and love them. They were to be provided with clothing and were tempted with new foods—citrus fruits, dates, and vegetables—which they would help the padres raise.

Indians flocked to the missions in great numbers. They gave up their tribal names and became known as the Mission Indians, and took up the Spanish way of life. Actually, they had placed themselves in a position of slavery. They were compelled to learn certain trades and to work at them around the missions. They were kept under rigid discipline which included corporal punishment and confinement if they tried to escape. And as for food—one pint of corn a day was considered adequate for a man, woman, or child who worked from morning prayers at dawn to dark.

Eventually, 20,000 to 30,000 Indians lived under the control of the Missions, which also controlled many miles of land, theoretically held in trust for the Indian people. In spite of the harshness of their existence, the Indians looked up to the padres with a childlike faith. For some individuals, there were strong bonds of affection.

During sixty-five years of Mission life, there were many deaths among the Indians, for disease ran high among them. As the population fell off, the Missions also declined and were abandoned when California became a possession of the Mexican government. Some of the land returned to the Indians, but most was carved up to form the great Mexican *ranchos*, and the Indian people scattered over the countryside. With their own culture shattered, and with little training in new skills, they became victims of starvation or lived in misery far worse than any they had known.

The northern tribes of California had no dealings with the Spaniards but carried on considerable trade with the Russians and other traders.

In 1848, Mexico ceded its California lands to the United States, which agreed to recognize Indian rights to the lands they occupied. The dominance of the Missions had reduced the Indian population by one-third. When the United States took over, there were 100,000 Indians and by the end of the nineteenth century there were only 17,000.

With the discovery of gold, California quickly became a state and more than 200,000 gold miners and settlers poured into the land. They looked upon Indian-held lands as probable gold fields, and while Indians tried to keep peace, the abduction of Indian women and children became common and "Indian hunts" were matters of organized killings of Indians for any fancied infraction of the white man's rules. Indians were prohibited from taking any action against a white man or even testifying in a court of law.

Then, California enacted a law for the settlement of private land claims. Most Indians could not read or write, and failure to present their land claims before the commission was considered forfeiture of them. Matters became so dreadful that finally a commission was established to set aside parcels of land for the few remaining Indians, and these were generally the poorest lands. No matter how poor, they were a boon to the people who had no place to go.

In 1905 public opinion began to be aroused in favor of the Indians, greatly influenced by the publication of the book *Ramona* by Helen Hunt Jackson. Although the characters were fictitious, the story was based on actual happenings and brought into focus the sufferings of the Indian people. Legislation was passed which appropriated funds to purchase many small tracts of land in central and south central California for the landless Indians. These purchases are the bulk of the Indian lands in that area today. In 1944 the Indians were awarded approximately $5 million, and in 1946 a $29 million-settlement was made against their claim to lands taken from them.

In 1911 a remarkable discovery took place in California. This was the discovery of an Indian, the last of his people, the Yahi, who had been in hiding for many years. He was thought to be forty-seven years old when he was found, and he was still living as his people had lived.

The Yahi were once a peaceful and gentle tribe in the Sacramento River valley. They had lived there all of three thousand years, hunting and fishing and carrying out their sacred rituals. When gold miners appeared in Yahi country, they asked no questions of the Indians but shot them down as they met. The settlers who followed fenced the land, killed off or frightened away the game, ploughed up the wild vegetables, and had little to do with the Indians who were in their way.

Food became scarce for the Yahi and so they took from the settlers what had been taken from them. Then the killing of Indians began in earnest as punishment. Yahi villages were attacked and wiped out. Women captives were sold as slaves and the men were hung. No mercy was shown to anyone.

The Yahis avenged themselves by raiding the settlers' stock and burning their cabins. They knew they fought a losing battle but they would rather die fighting than starve to death. Within ten years, most of the small tribe was wiped out.

By 1870, only fifteen Yahi survived a final Indian massacre. They disappeared and were never seen again. By 1899 only five of this group were left. These were Ishi, his mother, a girl cousin, an uncle, and a youth. They had successfully kept themselves hidden from white eyes and continued to live in the Yahi way.

In 1908, a party of engineers stumbled onto the hidden village of the five and removed all the stored food, baskets, tools, clothing, and hunting bows. The Indians had mysteriously vanished. If they returned, they would have nothing with which to sustain themselves. Ishi never saw his uncle or cousin again after the engineers had visited the village, although he searched for them for months. Then, his mother and the youth died, so he was completely alone in the hills— the very last Yahi. Half-dead from starvation, grief, and weariness, one day he collapsed, wanting to die. Instead, he woke to find himself surrounded by the hated white men, their guns pointed directly at him.

For awhile, Ishi was held in jail for his own protection. At first he could neither eat nor sleep, but soon he began to understand that he was not to be harmed. Slowly, he got used to being among white men. But he was the only Stone

Age Indian in all America—and what would happen to him?

One day Ishi was visited by a professor from the University of San Francisco who had made a study of the Yahi Indians and could speak some Yahi. The two were to become lifelong friends. Ishii agreed to go with the professor to San Francisco where he was given a comfortable room in the anthropology department at the university museum. He was fascinated by everything he saw or heard and not at all afraid of the strangeness of the city. He helped the museum anthropologists by recording his language and by telling them of Yahi customs. On Sunday afternoons, he appeared before the public and demonstrated how the Yahi had lived. So that he could be supported, he was put on the payroll as a janitorial assistant, and he took great pride in his job and in his salary, and in learning how to shop and to ride public transportation and find his way about. He made many friends, but none were so special as those of the museum staff. He enjoyed all the aspects of modern life, although tall buildings left him unimpressed. As for airplanes, he said that a hawk could fly better.

At one time he went with a museum party to his old home, demonstrating there all that he had told about and showing how the Yahi had been able to live so many years in hiding and how they hid. But he had no desire to stay where the memories were so unhappy and looked forward eagerly to the return to the museum—his "home."

Ishi died of tuberculosis in 1916. He was cremated, in Yahi tradition, with some acorn meal, his bow and arrows, tobacco, and a purse of personal treasures so that he would have a safe journey to his ancestors.

Ishi loved to give to his friends. He was kind to all and held no bitter feelings about all that had happened to him. He was greatly mourned by all who knew him.

❖   ❖   ❖

Although the Agua Caliente Indians are small in number, their reservation is the best known of the surviving Mission Indian communities. There are only about 168 members of the band whose ancestors were Cahuilla Indians. Their reservation comprises 32,000 acres surrounding the famous resort city of Palm Springs. Nearly 10.5 square miles lie within the city limits of Palm Springs, making the Indians the largest single landowner in this growing resort area. This is the richest block of real estate that California Indians hold. The balance of their land fans out across the desert in a checkerboard pattern, even mounting the sheer slopes of the San Jacinto Mountains.

The Hoopa Indians in the north have the largest reservation in the state of California. The Hoopa Reservation has more than two billion board feet of standing timber from which the Indians derive a continuing source of revenue. Modern methods and machinery are used by the Hoopa for the successful management of their forests.

One of the early chiefs of note in California was Solano of the Suisuns. He was over six feet tall and a man of keen intellect. When the Spaniards came, the Suisuns numbered about 40,000. Their villages were destroyed, and Solano was chosen to lead the Indians in a revenge attack. He decided, instead, that "brotherhood" was best and he cultivated the friendship of the newcomers and sought their help for his people. He realized that the Indians would only destroy themselves if they tried to engage in battle and fight so formidable a foe.

Solano frequented the Franciscan Mission when it was built, and he became a Catholic. He learned to read and write and was commissioned as a captain in the Mexican army. When he died, he was buried with great honors. There was a tremendous funeral and Indians came from miles around to attend.

There is a statue of Solano in the town of Fairfield. It is the only statue in the entire state which memorializes a specific Indian.

When the United States acquired the state of California, negotiations were held with the Indians, who relinquished all of their rights and title to the nearly 75,000,000 acres of California territory. They were guaranteed rights of perpetual use and occupancy to reservations, which were described in each treaty, totalling 8,518,900 acres. They were promised specific quantities of goods in large amounts, subsistence supplies, tools for farming, livestock and clothing, and the services of teachers, farmers, carpenters and other workmen. They were to receive everything necessary for their education and support, so that they could prepare themselves for complete independence. As has been stated, it was not until many years later that California Indians received any land or assistance at all.

The Bureau of Indian Affairs provides certain services for the California Indians, administering certain trust responsibilities. The Indian children attend public schools, and the state has assumed full responsibility for providing welfare services to nonreservation Indians. But gradually, the small *rancherias* are being withdrawn from all federal supervision, with title to the land and assets being turned over to the Indians.

TRIBES OF CALIFORNIA

Achomawi (Pit River) ("river")
Agua Caliente ("warm water")
Atseguis (Pit River)
Cahuilla
Chaushila
Chemehuevi
Chilula
Chimariko ("man")
Chumash
Costanos ("coastmen")
Diegueno
Esselen
Fernandeno
Gabrieleno
Hoopa (Hupa)
Juaneno
Kawia
Karok ("upstream")
Kato ("lake")
Konomihu
Lassik
Luiseno
Maidu ("person")
Mattole
Miwok ("people")
Mohave
Mono
Ohlone ("people of the west")
Okwanuchu
Olamentke
Patwin ("person")
Pomo
Salinan
Serrano ("mountaineers")
Shasta
Sinkyone
Suisun
Tolowa

Wailaki ("northern speech")
Wappo ("brave")
Washo ("person")
Whilkut
Wintun ("people")
Wishosk
Wiyou
Yahi ("person")
Yana ("person")
Yokuts ("people")
Yolo ("region thick with rushes")
Yuki ("strangers")
Yuma
Yurok

Major Linguistic Stocks
Athapascan
Chimarikan
Chumashan
Costanoan
Copehan
Esselenian
Kulanapan
Lutuamian
Moquelumnan
Pujunan
Quoratean
Salinan
Shastan
Shoshonean
Washoan
Weitspekan
Wishokan
Yanan
Yukian
Yuman

INDIAN RESERVATIONS IN CALIFORNIA

Colorado River (Chemehuevi, Mohave, Hopi, Navajo) — Riverside and San Bernardino counties (California), Yuma county (Arizona)

Fort Mohave — San Bernardino county (California), Mohave county (Arizona), Clark county (Nevada)

Fort Yuma — Imperial county (California), Yuma county (Arizona)

Hoopa Valley — Humboldt county

Palm Springs (Agua Caliente) — Riverside county

Tule River — Tulare county

Except for the above, there are no large settlements or Indian holdings in California. Indian lands are scattered over some 117 relatively small reserves, or *rancherias*, many of them individual Indian homesites. The greatest concentration is in Riverside and San Diego counties. The most populous communities are those of the Pit River people—the Achomawis and Atseguis (Atsugewi)—near Alturas.

Indians of the Northwest Coast

The vast Northwest area was originally occupied by many tribes, divided into two major and sharply differing cultures. In the dry uplands of eastern Washington and Oregon, a number of plateau tribes ranged. These were "horse Indians," somewhat similar to the Indians of the Plains, but, unlike the Plains groups, they were fishermen as well. West of the Cascade Mountains were those Indians whose lives centered around fish and forests. They fished the teeming rivers, especially for salmon, and hunted for game. At least fifty tribes lived among the rivers and bays of Washington and Oregon.

Farther to the north, the Indians were unlike any other Indians of America. Among them were found customs, crafts, art, and traditions completely distinctive and unique—and very strange. In some ways, customs were flavored with a touch of the Oriental, and the people were often Asiatic in appearance. Some had "Fu Manchu" mustaches, where in other parts of the country, Indians were seldom seen with hair growing on the face or body. Some of their clothing was similar to the mandarin robes of China, and carved wooden hats, like inverted wooden bowls, resembled the coolie hats of that Oriental country.

For ceremonial events, the leading families indeed resem-

163

bled the Chinese mandarins, dressing in long straight shifts, either woven with fantastic designs, or with these designs painted on them. Robes of beautiful, silver-frosted sea otter furs were worn, the inside tinted in a green color to match the green of the abalone shells used for ornamentation, and painted with the family crest. With this was worn a tall, wooden headdress decorated with flicker feathers. Sea lion whiskers at the top held a "nest" of bits of swans' down, and long strips of ermine fell down from the back like a train. As the wearer moved about, or bowed, the swans' down floated out and into the air like snowflakes.

In the rainy climate, the people did not otherwise wear clothing, except for poncho-like rain cloaks. After the coming of the traders, from whom the Indians obtained dark blue and red cloth, garments were made of the blue material, with crest designs cut from the red cloth stitched onto it and outlined with hundreds of tiny pearl buttons. In battle, the Northwest coast men wrapped themselves in armor made of wooden slats and wore a carved wooden headpiece, like knights of old.

These remarkable Indians, alone among all others, placed great value on the ownership and acquisition of private property and on the flaunting of wealth. But wealth was not money. It was those things which could be traded or given away at the great feasts called *potlatches.* At these feasts there was intense rivalry between families as to who could give the most. Many slaves were owned and the host of the potlatch would think nothing of putting a number of them to death, just to demonstrate that he was so wealthy he could afford to do something of the kind to impress his rivals.

In some groups it was the custom to charge an interest rate of 100 per cent on everything given. But all of the gifts, with their doubled interest, had to be returned to the giver at another potlatch before the year was out. To be deeply in debt was considered an honorable way of life. The children of a noble family could recite the family debts as other children today recite the multiplication tables.

In this culture, every single thing was owned, and there was a price for everything. Carving rights were owned, designs were owned, songs were owned, family crests were owned, the right to build a canoe was owned—and the skilled artisans who possessed these rights could command much payment for their services. Every inch of ground was owned, as well as the waters of the coast and the fishing stations and the berry patches. Only those who had ownership rights could go to any of these areas without permission.

The country where these Indians lived was mountainous and heavily wooded with trees so tall and thick that it was not possible to clear the land. The people lived along the sea coast and were true sea-rovers. They raised no crops and did no hunting except for the huge fish and mammals of the sea. Where the Plains Indians had the horse, the coast Indians had their great sea-going canoes in which they ranged the ocean, attacking villages and taking captives for slaves. They were master carvers and woodworkers and, with the crudest of tools, felled the giant trees, hewing from them the planks for their tremendous houses which could hold as many as 200 people, the 60-foot long canoes, and the tall totem poles, which are the tallest wood sculptures in the world. Everything was elaborately carved with complicated designs, from the poles which recorded family histories, to the smallest spoon. Wood was steamed and bent and formed into boxes or put to other possible use.

The totem pole carvers were trained for their craft from boyhood. They had to learn all the songs and dances and traditions of the tribe, since they would be making poles for different families. They could become as wealthy as the wealthiest of chiefs, for a good carver would be paid at least

$750 in goods for one pole. The best carvers could ask much more than this.

While a pole was being carved, a song writer created the songs and ceremonials which would be used at the feast and ceremony of raising the pole. He, too, would be paid for his work, for he not only wrote the songs and ceremonies, but gathered together the actors who would perform them and trained and rehearsed them for a number of months. Such rites had to be letter perfect. Hundreds of people would be invited, and each guest would bring relatives and slaves with him.

There was a ceremony for every stage of life and for every event in life. Actually, some were great dramatic presentations in which stories were acted out by many participants and in which the medicine men, or *shamen*, performed unusual feats of magic. Wonderful carved masks were worn in the ceremonies, some with moving parts and some with faces within faces, looking like unearthly creatures from a world unknown to man, as indeed they were. These were the representations of the mythical animal, bird, or fish ancestors from whom the people claimed descent and who had supposedly lived thousands of years ago.

The houses of the Northwest tribes were as unusual as the people. They were very large buildings because each house sheltered an entire family and all of its relations, even those related by marriage. The largest house could hold 600 people, and 200 was not an unusual number.

The doorway to a house was a large cedar post carved with the likeness of the family crest animal or creature. Entrance was through the mouth or stomach of the carving. Other posts carved from the huge trees stood at each corner of the building.

Inside the house, a series of smoothly planked wide steps or terraces led down to the center where, surrounded by a wooden floor, a fire blazed in a pit under a smoke hole. In a very large house there would be more than one fire. The terraces were divided into living compartments for the various family groups. There were sleeping benches but no other furniture. Woven cedar mats covered the floors. The most important families lived closest to the fire. The chief and his immediate family had their living quarters at the back of the house. No one went there unless sent for.

Russian sailors were the first whites to contact the peoples of Alaska—the Indians, Eskimos, and Aleuts, who are now grouped under the heading of Alaska Natives. The Russians enslaved the Natives, especially the Aleuts, and forced them to hunt sea otters, sailing as far as southern California and to Japan. The women were captured and the men were forced to buy back their families by continuing as hunters.

Unlike Indians elsewhere, the Alaska tribes were not pushed off their lands but retained a land base for survival. While in remote areas living is still very primitive, most have adjusted well to the modern way of life, for none have been untouched by the coming of the white man and the impact of progress.

In 1971, the United States passed the Alaska Native Claims Settlement Act, the largest cession of land to a group of native Americans in our history. The Act places about one-twelfth of Alaska into the hands of specially formed Alaska Native Corporations, unique in the records of solutions to aboriginal land claims. Organized on a regional basis, these will act as any business corporation, issuing stock, investing money, and conducting financial affairs for the villages in their areas. All in all, the Native people will get title to 40 million acres of land and, in addition, a $500 million federal appropriation and $500 million in mineral royalties.

In Alaska, the Athabascans (or Athapascans, spelled with the p as in the linguistic stock) are the most numerous and the most primitive of the tribes of Indians there. Living in the interior, they were a nomadic people who hunted the moose and caribou. Today, they live in log cabin villages, governed by a chief and council elected each year. The council members give many hours of direct community service to the tribe.

The men are excellent carpenters and make the most of what they have. In their country it takes months to build a cabin, for the logs must be cut, dragged long distances, and seasoned for a year. Weeks are spent in gathering moss to cover the roof, then tons of earth are lifted to the roof to be spread over the moss. The result is a snug, warm dwelling.

Summers are short in Athabascan country, and winter temperatures can drop to fifty below zero. This makes it difficult to obtain water, since streams freeze so quickly and thickly that hours of hacking are needed to break the ice to get to water level. Ice and snow must be melted for water on stoves made of empty oil drums.

The men still hunt wild game, but now depend more upon the river salmon for food. They weave fine willow traps to catch the fish. Children are taught to become skilled trappers at an early age.

The newest Commissioner of Indian Affairs, who is the fourth Indian to hold this office, is an Athabascan. Morris A. Thompson is from the village of Tanana. He is the youngest person ever to hold the office of Commissioner, coming to the position from the post of area director for Alaska for the Bureau of Indian Affairs.

Tlingit villages are run according to a traditional complicated social structure. The Tlingits were originally great traders, trading especially the small oily oolachon fish which were dried and burned to light the huge plank houses of the Indian people. The Tlingits were also great fighters, and defeated the Russians time after time with only their primitive weapons.

The famous Chilkat blanket, woven of mountain goat hair on a cedar warp, was one of their finest products. Every high-caste Tlingit was buried in one.

The Native peoples of Alaska have long participated in the legislative affairs of the state as members of the state legislature. Frank Peratrovich, a Tlingit Indian, was elected to the House of Representatives in 1944 and to the Senate in 1946. He was elected president of the Senate in 1961 and held this office longer than any other senator.

The Tsimpshians fled to Annette Island, which was given to them by the United States in 1887, to escape religious persecution in British Columbia. They are well-adjusted and well-integrated into the life of the state and take part in all of the social, economic, and political life.

Their large village of Metlakatla is run on a cooperative plan. A salmon cannery, the water system, and a sawmill are owned in common. Fishing boats and village stores are individually owned. A large landing field serving jet planes operates under lease on the island. Metlakatla has operated a hydro-electric power system since 1957, with annual profits running more than $100,000.

The Haida tribe is the smallest in number. In their original life, the Haidas were the finest of carvers, painters, canoe makers, and house builders. They are still noted for their fine carving. Totem pole carving is said to have originated among them.

Hydaburg, the chief Haida village, is a fairly modern town with substantial frame houses and a cooperative salmon cannery. Many of the Indians build and operate power fishing boats.

Chief It-in-sa was one of the wealthiest and most honored Haida chiefs of the nineteenth century. He was a staunch

defender of Haida customs and beliefs but he was friendly
to whites and, through his influence, a missionary came to
the tribe. Convinced that Indian ways must change, It-in-sa
set the example for his kinsmen. He said that change was a
challenge and that the Haidas must learn to adapt to the
change that was in store for them. First, with all members of
his family, he was baptized in the church. He gave up his
Indian name and became Albert Edward Edenshaw, named
for Prince Albert of England, because he, too, came from a
royal family. Then he gave up all his slaves and his Indian
style of dress. For formal occasions, he wore a silk top hat
with a Prince Albert style of clothing, and carried a gold-
headed cane. He sent the children of his family to school and
church, and the Haidas turned their backs on all carving.

But he continued to live in an Indian plank house, and
now and again he gave a potlach ceremony, even though
these were forbidden by law. So, when he died, no totem pole
was erected for him as would have been done for so great
a chief as he in olden times. But by then, many of the totem
poles had been torn down and destroyed, for the missionaries frowned upon them as heathen practices.

In 1926, the Tlingit community of Kake had accepted the
counsel of missionaries and burned an irreplaceable collection
of crest and story totem poles. They had done this with dignity, but with aching hearts, for the poles had great meaning.
They were never at any time worshipped as idols, but the
missionaries did not understand the place that the poles held
in the culture of the people. From then on, Kake was without a totem pole.

A few years ago, there was a revival of interest in Alaska's
Indian art and culture and a number of artists began to re-
produce carvings and paintings of native origin. With this
encouragement, the people of Kake decided that they would
build a totem pole that would be the tallest ever made. It

would be a towering 132 feet—not only the tallest, but the most expensive. The carving fee alone ran to $10,000 and this did not include several thousand dollars worth of donated effort by Alaska logging and shipping companies that helped to locate, cut, and transport one of the tallest red cedars in the northern forests.

It was planned that the pole would include both Haida and Tlingit figures. Ordinarily, it would contain only Tlingit carvings, but the people of Kake did not see this as just another pole. To them, it represented the reawakened heritage of Indians from one end of Alaska to the other. Family clan and village emblems representing every portion of southeast Alaska were also included. When the pole was completed, seventeen village leaders traveled more than 200 miles for the dedication. They were dressed in the wonderful old costumes and they performed age-old dances.

The great pole was then sent to Japan for display during Expo '70 before it was returned to Kake for erection. Since then, new poles have been erected by the Haida Indians in their village at Masset, British Columbia, with the proper ceremonies. Many of the thousand Indians who attended had never before seen a totem pole raised, or eaten at a potlatch.

"There is hope for the white man," the old chiefs say, "for now he is beginning to see the important things in life."

In the "lower states" of the Northwest, the Modoc tribe waged the last major Indian war with the United States in 1872–73. The Modocs lived in southwest Oregon, close to the California border. They were in frequent conflict with the whites coming in over the Oregon Trail, but in 1864 they joined with the Klamaths in ceding their territory. They moved to the Klamath Reservation, but were never happy there, for there was friction between the two groups. The Modocs made persistent efforts to return to their old home, and finally a chief known to the whites as Captain Jack led some to the California border and refused to return.

When attempts were made to force him to go back to the reservation, the Modoc War broke out. The Indians fled to the lava beds of northern California and for a number of months resisted any attempts to dislodge them. The lava beds were like a fortress, since they could not be penetrated except by the Indians, who knew every crook and cranny of them. Finally, a peace conference was held. Captain Jack asked three times that he and his people be allowed to stay in their homeland, and three times he was refused. Then, in a surprise move, two of the peace commissioners were killed and one was nearly so. Again the Indians fled to the lava beds and were only dislodged when cannon were brought. Captain Jack and his leaders were hanged.

The heroine of the Modoc troubles was Winema, a cousin of Captain Jack. When she was a very young girl, Winema earned her name of Strong-Hearted Woman because of acts of bravery unusual in one so young. At fifteen, she married a white miner and with her husband Frank settled down happily on a ranch where she began to learn "how white people live." She would teach all that she learned to her own people and she tried to keep friendly relations between white and Indian. Many times she averted bloodshed. She was helpful as an interpreter, especially during the negotiations which arranged for the Modocs to go to the Klamath Reservation.

When Captain Jack left with his band, Winema went to his camp at the risk of her life, and tried to reason with him. Jack turned his back on her to indicate that she was "dead to him" and that he would have no more to do with her. During the peace conference in which the two men were killed, Winema saved the life of Colonel Meacham, the third man who was so seriously injured. She got him safely away and nursed him carefully back to health. Meacham later wrote a book about her. Winema visited Washington and a great parade was held in her honor. A play was written about her and produced, and she played her own part. Touring the country in this play, she was treated everywhere as an honored citizen. Seventeen years after the Modoc War, she was given a pension of twenty-five dollars a month.

The Lummi Indians of Washington State have an unusual enterprise which is a pronounced success. The Lummis have built the first oyster hatchery in the Northwest and have spawned and set millions of oysters to grow on Lummi-built fiberglass rafts.

The tribe has pioneered the first red-algae harvest industry on the west coast and the first mechanized subtidal harvest system in the world. They have converted rainbow trout from fresh to sea water, and they are developing a new harvest system for marine bait worms. A major effort was the construction of a 4,000-foot sea dike to enclose four acres of fish and shellfish research ponds in Lummi Bay. All aspects of the aquaculture project are owned by the tribe, which has about 1,600 members.

In the two states of Washington and Oregon abundant timber stands are rich resources for some of the reservations. The tribes of these two states and Idaho own more than two million acres of commercial forest land with a total commercial timber volume of more than 20 billion board feet. The leaders in timber production are the Colvilles and Yakimas.

One of the most ambitious of tribal tourist enterprises is the mineral springs resort on the Warm Springs Reservation in Oregon. The tribe has invested more than one million dollars in their unique resort which boasts two swimming pools, one of Olympic dimensions, warmed by the waters of the hot springs. Visitors may stay in comfortable cottages or a motel, or in authentic Indian tipis.

TRIBES OF THE NORTHWEST COAST

(Alaska, Washington, Oregon, and into British Columbia)

Athabascan ("grass or reeds here and there")	Alaska
Ahtena	Alaska
Bella Coola	British Columbia
Cathlamet	Oregon
Cathlapotle	Washington
Cayuse	Washington, Oregon
Chasta (Shasta)	Oregon
Chehalis	Washington
Chetco ("close to mouth of stream")	Oregon
Chilluckkittequaw	Washington
Chimakum	Washington
Chinook	Washington
Clackamas	Oregon
Clallam ("strong people")	Washington
Clatsop ("salmon")	Oregon
Clowwewalla	Oregon
Colville	Washington
Comox	British Columbia
Coos (Kosan)	Oregon
Copalis	Washington
Coquille	Oregon
Cowichan	British Columbia
Cowlitz	Washington
Duwamish (Dwamish)	Washington
Haida ("people")	Alaska, British Columbia
Ingalik	Alaska
Kalapuya	Washington
Kalispel (Pend d'Orielles) ("ear drops")	Washington
Klamath	Oregon
Klikitat ("beyond")	Washington
Koyukon	Alaska
Kutchakuchin ("giant people")	Alaska
Kutchin ("people")	Alaska
Kwaialak	Washington

Kwakiutl ("beach on other side of river")	British Columbia
Kwalhioqua ("at a lonely place in the woods")	Washington
Lummi	Washington
Makah ("cape people")	Washington
Methow	Washington
Modoc ("southerners")	Oregon
Molala	Oregon, Washington
Multnomah	Oregon
Nehalem	Oregon
Nespelem	Washington
Nestucca	Oregon
Nez Perce ("pierced nose")	Washington, Oregon
Nisqually	Washington
Nooksack ("mountain men")	Washington
Nootka	British Columbia
Ochechote	Washington
Okanagon	Washington
Palouse (Palus)	Washington
Puyallup ("shadow")	Washington
Quileute	Washington
Quinault	Washington
Sahehwamish	Washington
Salish (Coast)	Washington
Samish	Washington
Sanpoil	Washington
Semiahmoo	Washington
Senijextee	Washington
Siletz	Oregon
Sinkiuse	Washington
Skagit	Washington
Skilloot	Washington
Skokomish ("river people")	Washington
Skoton	Oregon
Snohomish	Washington
Snoqualmie	Washington
Spokan (Spokane)	Washington
Squaxon	Washington
Suquamish	British Columbia
Swinomish	Washington

Takelma ("those dwelling along the river")	Oregon
Tanana	Alaska
Tenino	Oregon
Tillamook	Oregon
Tlingit (Tlinkit) ("people")	Alaska, British Columbia
Tsimpshian ("people inside of Skeena River")	Alaska
Tulalip	Washington
Tututni	Oregon
Twana ("portage")	Washington
Tyigh	Oregon
Umatilla	Oregon
Umpqua	Oregon
Walla Walla ("little river")	Washington, Oregon
Wasco ("cup or bowl of horn")	Oregon
Watlala (Cascade)	Oregon
Wenatchee ("river spreading from a canyon")	Washington
Willopah	Washington
Yakima ("runaway")	Washington
Yamel	Oregon
Yaquina	Oregon
Yonkalla	Oregon

Major Linguistic Stocks
Athapascan
Chimakuan
Chimmesyan
Chinookan
Kalapooian
Kitunahan
Koluschan
Kusan
Lutuamian
Salishan
Shahaptian
Skittagetan
Takilman
Waiilatpuan
Wakashan
Yakonan

INDIAN RESERVATIONS OF THE NORTHWEST COAST

WASHINGTON

Colville	Okanogan and Ferry counties
Spokane	Stevens county
Yakima	Yakima county
Kalispel	Pend Oreille county
Ozette (Makah)	Clallam county
Makah	Clallam county
Quileute	Mason county
Quinnault	Mason county
Tulalip (Snohomish)	Snohomish county
Muckleshoot	King county
Puyallup	Pierce county
Nisqually	Thurston county
Chehalis	Mason county
Squaxon	Mason county
Skokomish	Mason county
Lummi	Whatcom county
Swinomish	Skagit county
Port Angeles (Clallam)	Clallam county

OREGON

Umatilla (Cayuse, Umatilla, Walla Walla)	Umatilla county
Warm Springs (Wasco, Warm Springs, Paiute)	Jefferson, Wasco counties
Fort McDermitt (Paiute, Shoshone)	Malheur county

ALASKA

There are no reservations in Alaska. Native life is organized around various villages, of which there are a great number.

Non-reservation Communities

OREGON

Alsea, Molalla, Umpqua	Lane, Douglas, Curry counties
Klamath	Klamath county
Western Oregon Indians	Over large coastal area

Indians of Canada

There was much overlapping of tribes across the Canadian border, but there were also very many tribes with their own Canadian identity. In eastern Canada, a number of tribes removed there from New England, seeking the protection of the French or of the British after the American Revolution. Some Plains tribes frequently crossed over into Canada on hunting forays, and there were a few living there as permanent residents. After the Custer battle, some of the Sioux under Sitting Bull took refuge in Canada, but did not remain there. Some tribes of Alaska are found in British Columbia or in the northwest part of the country. The Iroquois and some of the central and Plains area tribes lived in both countries.

Listed here are major Canadian groups. Not included are the tribal divisions and the numerous small bands scattered across Canada with, or without, tribal identification. The Coast Salish, for example, included many tribes. The Cowichan, a division of the Coast Salish, was comprised of a large number of tribes, most of them quite small but some, such as the Nanaimo, with important status in their locality.

The cultural patterns for tribes in Canada are usually extensions of those found in the United States for each given

territory or area. Those with an asterisk were not native to
the area.

EASTERN WOODLANDS
 *Abenaki
  Beothuk ("men")
  Cree
  Huron
 *Iroquois (Mohawk, Onondaga)
 *Malecite
  Micmac ("allies")
  Montagnais ("mountaineers")
  Naskapi
  Neutrals
  Ojibwa (Chippewa) ("puckered")
  Tobacco (Tionontates) ("where the mountain stands")

PLAINS
  Assiniboine
  Blackfeet
  Gros Ventre
  Plains Cree
  Sarcee (Sarsi) ("not good")
  Sioux

WESTERN CANADA
  Carrier
  Chilcotin ("people of young man's river")
  Kootenay (Kutenai)
  Nicola
  Tahltan
  Interior Salish

PACIFIC COAST
  Bella Coola
  Coast Salish
  Comox
  Cowichan
  Haida
  Kwakiutl
  Nootka

Suquamish
Tlingit (Tlinkit)
Tsimpshian

MACKENZIE AND YUKON RIVER BASINS
Athabascan
Beaver
Chipewyan ("pointed skins")
Dogrib
Hare
Kutchin (Loucheux)
Nahani (Kaska)
Sekani ("people of the rocks")
Slave (Slavey)
Tagish
Yellowknife

Major Linguistic Stocks
Algonquian
Athapascan
Beothukan
Iroquoian
Haida
Kootenayan
Salishan
Siouan
Tlingit
Tsimshian
Wakashan

In Tribute

From this summary of Indian tribes around the country, it will be seen that there are still many Indians of great variety. It is believed that there are more than when Columbus arrived, although there are fewer tribes.

In the Indian past, there were those who farmed, fished, hunted, and wandered. There were those who built temples and those who built nothing. There were those who were advanced or who advanced very quickly with contact with new ways. And there were those who lived simply, with little change in their pattern of life.

It can also be seen that Indians are people of intelligence, creativeness, inventiveness, and adaptability. In order to survive the elements and the harsh conditions of the stark land, to maintain themselves and to protect themselves, they had to have these qualities. They had to be physically strong, mentally alert, and flexible with the changing moods of nature. They could not be an idle people, for animals did not wait for the lazy hunter and plants did not grow without patient care.

They were also a kind and generous people, sharing whatever they had with friend or stranger. They had imaginative powers that could make their words and thoughts poetic, and they were artisans of great ability. In addition to our great and beautiful land, which the Indians loved and cherished, Americans are deeply indebted to the Indian people for these qualities, and for the many contributions which came from them.

As proof of their creativeness and skill, the Indians had three kinds of crops—those developed from wild growths and cultivated, those taken over from wild growths without change, and those that were used in their wild state, not only for food but for medicines and household materials. A very great part of the food supply of the world had its origin with the American Indian. At least four-sevenths of all the agricultural products of this country are from Indian gardens. Of these, corn, or maize, is the most important. It has been said that without this one plant alone, the people of the world would starve. The Indians had a number of varieties of corn, including popcorn, and an early form of Cracker Jack. For this, hot maple syrup was poured over popcorn.

The next important food crop was potatoes. These were taken by the Spaniards to Europe where they became a principal food. They were brought back to this country by the colonists, who called them "Irish potatoes."

Tobacco, one of the world's most important commercial crops, was grown by Indians long before the "discovery" of America. The Indians rolled the leaves into rough cylinders, or tubes, and smoked them. They also smoked the leaves in pipes which they invented. But tobacco was a sacred plant, and because of its ceremonial use, few tribes smoked for pleasure.

Until Columbus came, cotton was unknown to the world except for a short staple growth found in India and Abyssinia. The long staple cotton of Egypt and the United States must be credited to Indians who developed it from a small, wild plant.

Rubber was another native crop that became highly important. And among the drugs of major significance that came from the Indian plants are digitalis, quinine, cocaine, and curare.

Everything in nature was put to use and nothing was wasted or willfully or wantonly destroyed. Conservation was practiced and animals were hunted for food and clothing only to meet the needs of the people—never for sport.

The canoe, snowshoes, the kayak, and the toboggan are all inventions of the Indian which are still used as they were originally designed.

Our main highways follow Indian trails and many of our large cities are built on the sites of Indian villages.

Indians have fought in all of the wars in which we have been engaged, from the American Revolution on down. They fought with bravery and distinction and have risen to high ranks in all branches of service. Several have won the Congressional Medal, given only for the most outstanding deeds of bravery. No group ever equaled the services of the Navajos in World War II who were used by the Marines for sending codes in their native language. These messages could not be translated by either German or Japanese, and the Navajo "code talkers" were the best-kept secret of the war.

Indians are found today in all vocations and there is hardly a profession which does not have some Indian representation. In military science, Alvin Bearskin, a Wyandot, is an aerospace technician who evaluates the design and operational function of equipment taken by the astronauts on moon landings.

With our environmental problems, we are beginning to understand that in this area we had much to learn from the Indians, and they still can teach us. Working together in cooperation, all Americans will gain, and Indians will not only build their own economies for Indian benefit, but will continue to forge ahead to a new stake and place in America.

Index

Only those tribes discussed in the text are indexed. For others, consult the lists of tribes following each geographical section. Lists of reservations, non-reservation communities, and linguistic stocks also follow each geographical section. See entries below: Tribes, Reservations, Non-reservation communities, Linguistic stocks, or the particular geographical location.

THE AUTHOR

Marion E. Gridley has devoted a lifetime to study and work with American Indians. She has been closely associated and identified with Indian affairs since her girlhood and is the author of twenty published books on Indian subjects. She is the originator of the Indian Achievement Award, presented annually to an Indian individual for accomplishment and humanitarian service, and since 1952 has published *The Amerindian,* a bimonthly periodical devoted to Indians on the current scene, Indian history and personalities. In 1970, she was cited by President Richard M. Nixon for her services to Indians through this publication.

She is an adopted member of two tribes, the Omaha and Winnebago, and was given the name of "Little Moonbeam" by the Omaha and "Glory of the Morning" by the Winnebago. In 1965, Miss Gridley received the Woman of the Year Award of the Illinois Woman's Press Association, and her books have received a number of state and national awards. She lives in Chicago.